FETCHING MILLION$

SECRETS FROM A SUCCESSFUL TRADE SERVICES BUSINESS OWNER

TOM HOWARD

MVHL

MVHL

New York | Los Angeles | London | Sydney

ISBN: 979-8-88581-181-1 Hardback
ISBN: 979-8-88581-182-8 Paperback
ISBN: 979-8-88581-183-5 eBook
Library of Congress Control Number:2024927326

DISCLAIMER

Tom Howard was an employee of ServiceTitan Inc. at the time this book was written and published; however, this book was not written on behalf of ServiceTitan Inc. and all of the ideas and recommendations put forth in this book are his own and do not represent ServiceTitan Inc.

DEDICATION

This book is dedicated to the people that have made this all possible for me. Joe Steinmetz, my high school HVAC teacher that taught me the trades at a young age. Micah Ames, my first boss in the trades who taught me the ropes when it came to small business. Bryan Lee, who taught me that a trades business can be more than a two-truck operation. Ara and Vahe who built an incredible software platform that made scaling to large sizes in the trades possible. All the partners at Fetch-a-Tech. I wouldn't have made a single penny on this deal without them. Gerry, Brent, Dennis, Dan, Collin and Trevor plus the employees that all contributed at Fetch. I get to take a lot of credit because I wrote the book and I am on stage a lot but they were the ones that actually made things happen. They truly deserve the credit.

CONTENTS

INTRODUCTION

I wrote this book to show what's possible in the trades. I also want to point out in this book that there isn't any magic to becoming successful and a multi-millionaire in is industry. In fact, anyone can do the same thing. You may have already done it. For all of you that haven't done it, I hope after reading this book, you walk away realizing that you can. For those of you that have done it, I hope to be able to entertain you with some of the stories about our endeavor.

In this book, I pull away the curtains and show what the team at Fetch-a-Tech did, and I'm going to do it in a way that you can copy all or some of what we did. I was going to share with you the month-by-month financials as well as the commentary to explain them but after selling the company, I had to sign an NDA restricting a lot of what I would have wanted to share. As I am writing this, I am in the process of selling my next large company and I won't sign a non-disclosure so I can be free to share all the data with you. I'm doing all of this because I truly want you, especially if you're in the trades, to be able to use the ideas that have helped me become successful. After all, many of the ideas that my team and I are sharing came from others anyway. Well, almost all of the ideas I have had have come from people that were generous enough to help me.

Another goal of this book is to give those who make their living from the trades, as well as the trades they represent, the positive recognition that they deserve.

Anyone who has been in the trades for longer than 10 minutes has probably felt looked down upon or has felt underestimated and even under appreciated at one time or another. It could have happened because you looked dirty when you walked into a restaurant on your lunch break after a rough day of crawling and pulling ductwork under a house, or when someone asks you what you do for a living. When you tell them that you work on installing and repairing garage doors, you can tell by the look on their faces that some just assume you live well below the poverty line. How wrong they are!

I didn't realize how overlooked the trade services were until I was in an airport and looking through magazines for something to read on the plane. I like the old-fashioned way of holding magazines in my hands when I read them. I would always pull Entrepreneur and Inc. Magazines, along with a few others, hoping to find nuggets I could use because I always saw my fellow business owners as entrepreneurs because that's what they are. But I was having a hard time finding any articles for business owners outside the tech industry, so I found myself no longer buying those magazines.

I understand that those magazines are for-profit businesses and don't blame them for writing to meet their reader's desires. But I want to change that. I want the world to realize there are even some people who have made more by selling their trades businesses than even the $175.8 million that Elon Musk made when he sold PayPal. I want the world to see how lucrative trade service businesses can be. When that happens, more people will be interested in pursuing careers in the trades. More than ever, young men and women will be knocking on the doors of our shops wanting to get into these businesses. That should lead to more banks and investors willing to fund new and even innovative projects in our space. When those changes happen, we will finally get the respect that is due those in the trades. That's my dream, and I'm sticking to it! I'm proud of what I do, and I want you to be proud too. This book is my way of sharing what I've learned. And by the end, you'll know the story behind the title, "Fetching Millions."

Finally, to reinforce that this is about elevating the trades and helping people who work there, 100% of the profits from this book will be donated to charities related to the trades.

Chapter One

MY BACKGROUND

I've been a very lucky man and there is no doubt that luck helped speed up the timeline on some of the achievements I'll be sharing and discussing in this book, but it doesn't mean if you don't have the same luck, that you can't do the same, or greater things.

When I was a kid, my mother moved around a lot due to her job, and my first big break in the HVAC industry came right after my mom moved to Southern New Hampshire when I was fifteen years old. That's when I got my first job in the trades working for a refrigeration mechanic who lived a few miles away. I worked for him after school and on the weekends cleaning the shop and doing menial tasks.

I was also incredibly fortunate and lucky because the high school for the area we moved to was Pinkerton Academy. It offered advanced placement classes in Math, Science, English and other classes as well as courses in five different languages. But what was really cool and remarkable for me was that they taught the trades for students who wanted to go in that direction.

I was making $6 an hour, so I told my boss about the classes to see if he would give me a raise. He said he'd give me a one dollar raise if I got into the Heating, Ventilation and Air Conditioning class at Pinkerton Academy and another dollar per hour if I got my EPA (U.S. Environmental Protection Agency) license. At that time, I was pretty sure anyone who made $8 an hour was basically a millionaire. I was going to do it.

I was able to take air conditioning and heating classes during my junior and senior years, something I wouldn't have been able to do at the public high school I would have been attending where we had previously lived in California. I was also in a couple of advanced placement classes including statistics, which would come in handy later, but the trades classes made the real difference in my life. I left high school with not only my EPA license, which was pretty easy to get, but with several other certifications as well from various agencies.

I look back now and wonder how different my life would have been if I hadn't been able to take those trades classes. I am very grateful that those classes were available. This was a public high school, and I owe the New Hampshire public school system a debt of gratitude for that training.

The best part to me though, at the time, was the money. Because I was putting the money I was earning in the bank, when I finished high school, I had managed to save the equivalent of about $5 million. Actually, it was more like $10 thousand. But back then at eighteen, with ten grand in the bank, I thought I was a millionaire!

My parents were certain I was going to spend it on attending college, but I had a slight detour in mind. I joined the Church of Jesus Christ of Latter-Day Saints, which is also known as the Mormon Church. I ended up spending the entire $10,000 going on a two-year mission to Hungary. When I made the decision, neither of my parents were members of the church, so they weren't too enthusiastic. Ok, they were bewildered. My mother became a member later, but when I got home, my dad said he wasn't going to give me money for school after the way I had spent the $10,000 I had saved. I knew my mom didn't have much, so, I had to figure out what to do next. At the time, my plan was to go to college, but it looked as if it would be up to me to pay for it. Again, the trades were there for me. Those of you who are in the trades know that when you have the right skills, getting a job isn't that difficult.

I ended up working for a couple of HVAC companies while I attended college for finance. At that time, I was biased against the trades and told myself that I wasn't going to work in the trades forever. It was just going to be a way to fund my college education. That's right back then, even I was dead set against working in the same trades I'm trying to attract youth to today.

I went to community college for a couple of years at Fresno City College in California, which was cheap, and then I got an academic scholarship to Brigham Young University in Utah to finish my degree in Finance. I paid for all of it with jobs in the trades. I was even married with a baby when my wife and I graduated, and we were able to do it all without school loans because of the trades.

After college, I was making a lot more in the trades than I was in the finance industry. I ended up going back to the trades. I got a job as General Manager at a company I had worked for during community college, Lee's Accu- tech Service, Inc. in Fresno, California. When I got back to Lee's and had been the General Manager for a few months, The Lee family decided to sell the business to me. At the time, Lee's was a small business, around $1.6 million in sales, but it was as big as I could handle at the time. Bryan Lee gave me the opportunity to buy it without me putting up money up front. I paid him monthly installments.

Finding a way to purchase someone else's business was a big step for me on my road to those first tens of millions. For me, buying Lee's sent me on my way and I could fill a whole book about what happened there next. I probably will write that one in the future by the way. Today, Lee's completed over 100 million in Revenue in 2024. It grew well and I love the team there, but this book is about Fetch-a-Tech in Las Vegas and it's turnaround.

Let's fast forward a little bit. After Lee's of Fresno, I bought a few other businesses with partners, one in Beverly Hills, one in Phoenix, one in Los Angeles, two businesses in Sacramento which are branded as Lee's.

I also bought a pest control company in Fresno called Dustin Pest Control, and a couple other small things that I probably shouldn't have bought. I won't list them here.

All those businesses are running on a software called ServiceTitan®, and in late 2019, I was asked to work for ServiceTitan. I knew the founders and they were willing to put up with my antics and we agreed to do it. We also agreed that I could keep my businesses as long as I disclosed which ones I owned and couldn't have access to a competitor's data. In exchange, I would represent contractors at the table in executive meetings. I loved working for them, but it took a ton of time. Since it was my full-time job and I had to move to Glendale, California to live near the ServiceTitan headquarters, my businesses have to run without me. I would take my business meetings on Zoom starting early in the morning around 5:30 or 6:00 am and then switch to ServiceTitan around 8:00 or 9:00 am.

I am proud to share that I am lucky enough to have four wonderful sons. Those boys keep me going and help drive me to set an example for them. Running businesses and working for ServiceTitan and making sure to spend time with them was rough. They mean the world to me. I made it work.

This was where I was in my life and work when the Fetch-a-Tech opportunity came along. At first, it looked more like a dumpster fire than an opportunity. But it would become one of the most enjoyable and fulfilling opportunities I have ever had.

Chapter Two

THE DUMPSTER FIRE

Gerry is a good friend of mine. We first met in Las Vegas at a dinner that I had been invited to by Ismael Valdez from Nexgen Heating and Air of Anaheim, California. That night I also met two brothers, Travis and Tyler Ringe, who had a shop called Pro-skill in Phoenix that they would later sell for tens of millions of dollars to Service Champions South. But at the time, they were just two brothers hustling to turn a big corner in their business.

After dinner, we all went out for a walk around Las Vegas and spent a couple hours talking about the HVAC industry. Travis and Tyler knew their margins, and their growth trajectory. They were smart and knew where they wanted to grow to. They didn't quite know how to get there yet, but they were on their way. Gerry, on the other hand, was a different story.

Before I say anything else, let me preface this with telling you that Gerry will be an ongoing character in this book, and you will see that he was absolutely critical to the whole story. Gerry had started a company in Phoenix and another one in Las Vegas at almost the same time. He didn't get one running that well before moving on to the next one. As anyone who has run a remote operation knows, you must really have things dialed in before trying to pull that off. But that didn't seem to matter much to Gerry. He was a fun-loving creative type who was always trying new things, and he was in love with all the new ideas in the industry. I appreciated his optimism, even if it was blind optimism. I could tell by the way Gerry was talking that the Ringe brothers were on a whole other level, so I focused most of my efforts on learning everything that they were doing. We would later work together on some things. But I also made friends with Gerry, and we would keep in touch.

Over the next year, Gerry would call me and ask for advice. I found out from the Ringe brothers that Gerry called everyone, every day, for everything. That part of him started to drive me nuts, but it would also become a huge asset to him. The problem was, Gerry wouldn't implement most of the things people told him to do. He would try to do a lot of them, and they wouldn't be completed for one reason or another. He has ADHD worse than I do, which is saying a lot, and is pretty proud of it. It is his secret weapon sometimes but if you have severe ADHD and don't have people around you that help you stay focused and really execute, it can be rough. The world is filled with people that want to be successful that attend conferences regularly and hear a ton of ideas but never execute. I call these people the dreamers of our industry. I see them over and over again going to the same conferences and listening to the same classes. When they are there, they dream about all the great things that they are going to do with their businesses. Then they go home and don't execute anything.

Here is the thing, there are very few new ideas out there. There aren't any silver bullets that will revolutionize your business and make you millions of dollars overnight. You can get enough ideas at almost any conference to make you tens of millions of dollars. The only difference between those that are wealthy and those that aren't at those conferences is just execution. That's it. If you are a dreamer, I have a piece of advice for you. At your next conference, try to get one or two ideas from the conference. Make sure that they will have an impact on your business and drop all the other ideas. Go back and focus and make sure you implement those two things at your business and make sure its sustainable. Don't try to implement twenty things. If you do, almost none of them will stick. Then, don't attend another conference until you have completed those two things. Then do it again at the next conference. One or two well implemented ideas are far more valuable than twenty that aren't implemented.

Anyway, Gerry asked me to travel to Phoenix to look at his operation. At this point, I was consulting for the Ringe brothers and needed to be in town anyway. When I dropped by Gerry's office he asked if I would be interested in partnering in his business. I looked around and told him "no." I was a jerk about it. I said, "Gerry, this place is a dumpster fire. You need to just let it go. It would be cheaper to start over."

I didn't want anything to do with it but I told him what I would do. I would, terminate a lot of employees and throw out a lot of stuff.

He took my advice, and he did do that.

I left that day and just shook my head. I simply didn't have the time to work on something like that. Then, Gerry invited me to see his Las Vegas operation, which was less of a disaster, but it was still pretty bad. Gerry had just hired a General Manager, Dennis. Gerry had told be about what a great hire Dennis was and when I met him, I thought Gerry was right. I realized that If Dennis had the resources he needed, he could do big things. No business operator is good at everything but all are good at something or they wouldn't be in business. Gerry was and is really good at connecting with people in the industry. He knew Dennis and hired him and you will see, his connections will keep making things happen over and over and over again in this book.

Unfortunately, the employees didn't have clear direction in their work. If they didn't like what Dennis was doing, they would call Gerry and Gerry would take their call. That undermined whatever Dennis the GM was doing. However, Gerry felt justified because, in some cases, Gerry's idea was right. But in other cases, he was probably wrong. The issue is that any time you do this, the GM doesn't feel empowered, and it kills his motivation. When that happens, the company can't move forward. Gerry wasn't doing it on purpose, but it was happening none the less, and it led to a totally inefficient and ineffective business.

This was a big lesson that I had to learn for myself at my other companies. If you own a business, this is one of the biggest lessons that will help you scale. I can't think of anything more important for scalability than EMPOWERING YOUR PEOPLE. It doesn't matter what position they are in; set targets they must hit and boundaries that they have to stay within and then get out of their way. Do not override what they do unless it breaks a boundary such as any ethical, legal, or safety requirements that they have to take into account and even then, bring it up with them directly if it does. Don't go over their head in front of everyone. If they aren't hitting their targets or their goals, then coach them on how to get there or, eventually, replace them, but do not go around them and change things. I'll discuss more about these issues later in this book.

Gerry and I continued talking and I helped with some things here and there. He wasn't paying me because I never asked him for money. I was just helping him as a friend, but after a while, I started getting tired of taking his calls.

I felt like Gerry wasn't listening anyway and he wasn't implementing what I asked him to do. At least, that's how I felt.

Gerry had also some positive things going on though. Remember how he called everyone in the industry every day? It was part of his ADHD I think. Well, that pays off big when you're looking to buy companies in your area. Those daily calls provided Gerry with incredibly valuable information. When people want to get out, you can usually get a decent deal. One guy was looking to dump his plumbing business called Priority services. It was a small four- or five-person operation. Gerry's main business in Las Vegas was called ACLV and only did air conditioning. By acquiring Priority Service, Gerry would be able to offer both plumbing and HVAC services. Plus, his General Manager, Dennis, had a background in plumbing, which made it an even more positive addition. It caught my ear and got me interested in Gerry's business.

We might have given Gerry a lot of garbage and teased him a lot and called his business a dumpster fire but at the end of the day, the deal with Priority and the entire future deal worths tens of millions would have never happened without his phone calls and all his connections, something that will come up time and again as our story continues.

There was a lot to clean up as Priority Plumbing and ACLV combined their operations. The financials were a mess at both businesses, with cash being disbursed and inadequately tracked. Before Gerry bought it, the General Manager of the plumbing business shut the phones off at 4:00 pm so the office could do yoga together. I am not kidding. Customers could have been calling with flooding in their house and no one was going to answer the phone due to their 4:00 pm Yoga session. Gerry and I were both shocked when we heard that one. Additionally, the phone system had been changed multiple times in one year and the office staff was having tons of trouble trying to figure out how to use it. Calls were being dropped, but no one really knew why.

I showed up one day in Vegas when their best installer walked in four hours late. I was stunned. Dennis asked him where he was and why he was late. "I was up until 11 pm doing side work. Give me a break," he said.

For some reason, he felt that this was an acceptable excuse. The everyday operations were a mess. It was obvious that Dennis was frustrated because he was working on getting things turned around, but the burden was heavy.

With the purchase of the new company, and Dennis working on major issues, it seemed like the dumpster fire was still burning, even if the flames seemed smaller than before. It was early 2021 and Gerry had asked me again if I wanted to partner in the Las Vegas business. I said that I still wasn't sure yet. However, I was thinking about how to turn that company around. I just didn't have all the pieces yet.

Unfortunately, Gerry owned an online business called AC for Less. It was probably the worst business name you can have if you are trying to sell a premium product at a decent margin. But a lot of the customers in his large database came in from that AC for Less online business. But I wasn't sure we could work with that.

The next problem was Gerry himself. He was a good creative guy, but not a manager and in my experience, owners like that usually wouldn't get out of the way. Their egos wouldn't let them. However, the cool thing with Gerry was that as much as I beat on him, he really didn't have much of an ego when it came to being willing to get out of the way. I was really surprised when he said that he was willing to do just that. This acquisition probably would have failed if Gerry wasn't as humble as he was. He heard the advice loud and clear and got out of the way. Looking back now, I can see how awesome Gerry really was. He simply would not stop. When he wanted something, he would keep pushing for it. When I couldn't see the value in things, he could. He kept calling me. His perseverance combined with his humility and friendliness with almost everyone in the industry made this whole deal possible.

I was still on the fence about what to do when something amazing happened. Fortunately, Gerry came through again. He brought in one of the best salespeople I've ever met

Chapter Three

THE TIPPING POINT

That addition of a terrific sales person I told you about happened after, soon after one morning, when I got a frantic call from Gerry. He told me that a guy named Brent Buckley had just quit his job. Brent was on track to do $7 million in sales in Las Vegas just by himself. Gerry was more excited than an eight-year-old on Christmas morning. He wanted me to meet Brent and said that if we could get him on the team, it would really come together. I was skeptical, but I wanted to meet this guy. Anyone that can sell $7 million in a year is good in my book. Even though I was still on the fence, Gerry and I had a loose agreement that I would partner with him once I felt the opportunity was good enough. Having Dennis as General Manager to lead and execute definitely helped, but we still needed a great salesperson. The Las Vegas operation was still a disaster, and you can't attract top talent with an operation that is a mess.

Early in my career, when I owned my first business in the middle of the great recession, I felt like the way to make sure we could pay the bills was to avoid spending money on anything. It worked to a point, but the office looked moderately ok. What I realized later was that you set a standard for your employees when you set up your office. If there is junk in your warehouse, it sends a message that it's ok to have junk in your truck. When you have tears in your carpeting, you send the message that it's ok to have tears in your uniforms that customers might eventually see. When you show up and want a premium price for your product, you can't show up with a truck with junk in it, and tears in your uniform. You must present well.

What I also found is that the impression your office makes when a potential hire walks in matters to them. You can't attract top talent with subpar office conditions. I am not saying you need gold toilets in your bathroom, but you need to make sure your employees know you care about your presentation. They won't take you seriously if you don't take yourself seriously.

So, get rid of the junk. I promise you, those old parts sitting on the shelf in the warehouse are not helping you. If it's there and not tracked, when someone is in the field and needs one, they won't know to even call the office to get it because they won't know it's there. Plus, the supply house is probably closer. They are just going to go get it from the supply house anyway. That leaves the part on your shelf, collecting dust in perpetuity and sending a negative message to your whole staff that it's OK to collect garbage. Before you know it, you are ordering more shelves to store more garbage that you are ever going to use. Just let it go.

I can't tell you how many times I have bought a small business, and the owner tries to sell me his inventory. I usually give him or her something for it just to make them feel better, but the first thing I do when buying the shop is throw all that stuff in the dumpster. They are usually shocked to see me do it, but I can't let their bad ideas dictate how we will be moving forward.

At any rate, I couldn't have Brent see this place in its current state. Even if we got rid of all the office junk and the junk in the warehouse, he could still see the inefficient processes in the office. I called Brent and invited him to my shop in Fresno. I had a decently run operation there. It's true that it had its own pitfalls and, trust me, I have shortcomings as well, but it was in better shape than the other operation. Brent came out to Fresno, and we chatted a lot. He looked around the operation and he liked it, but he told me that there was no way he was moving to Fresno, and he knew that I basically had nothing for him in Las Vegas. By that time, he was meeting with a lot of different companies courting him. One of them was in Southern California. I drove him down there and dropped him off at that shop.

The next morning, he called to tell me he had made a deal with that shop in SoCal and that he was going to open a branch for them in Las Vegas. I felt like the best thing for him was not to come work with us at the time, and picking someone else made more sense. I wished him the best of luck. I had recommended a couple others to him as well, so we stayed on good terms.

It only took a few weeks, though, and that other deal he made for himself had fallen through. I felt bad for Brent, but at the same time, we now had a chance again to get him. There was only one problem: Gerry and I still had a dumpster fire on our hands. And, to get Brent, all the other shops were offering him equity in their businesses. Some were offering up to 50%. If we did that, then Gerry and I would be left with 25% each. Gerry and I knew that a great sales agent was essential to the success of this business, so we were willing to make that deal. This was a longshot to get Brent, but we had a shot.

I talked to Brent and discussed our long-term plans and the ideas we had. Gerry and I played the only card we had, the large active customer databases we had developed. The other shops were thinking about opening operations for the first time in Las Vegas and starting from scratch, while we had tens of thousands of people in a database. Most of them were used to paying super low prices, but we may have left that part off during the discussion with Brent. It didn't matter, because Brent knew it right away and even brought it up to us. We also pointed to the fact that we had already done it—built a successful company—in Fresno. With all that information, Brent got interested, and we went to him with an offer of 30% of the business. That left 30% for me, 30% to for Gerry and 10% for Dennis.

Some of you may be thinking why would I give away so much of the business? Keep in mind, it wasn't my business yet, and I didn't pay for it. It hadn't made any money from it either in years, and we needed to get this thing off the ground. Giving away equity seemed like the best way to make that happen. Gerry was more than happy to give up all that equity because he saw the potential of what could be if we had the right team in place. Moreover, I had a full-time job at ServiceTitan, and several other businesses to run. Mainly, I couldn't afford to be stingy with the equity in the deal and lose a team that could deliver for us.

Brent ended up taking the deal, and Gerry and I were stoked. But we still had a dumpster fire to put out. That would be hard, but it had to be done.

It was late August 2021 when we made this very informal agreement. We had a lot of the right people on the bus, but the bus wasn't going anywhere quite yet. Still, this was the tipping point, and the wheels would start rolling pretty quickly after that. Brent would become one of the top salespersons, if not the top salesperson, in the country the next year. Besides Gerry and Dennis, Brent was another person who, without him, the Fetch deal wouldn't have happened like it did. We all would have made one quarter, or less, of what we ended up making if we didn't get Brent. He was a critical piece of the puzzle.

Chapter Four

GETTING ROLLING

Now we had the right team. I'd heard about the importance of getting the right people on the team a million times before, but I never really understood just how true it really was until now when I was experiencing it first-hand. I had always believed in having really good people and that the better people you have, the more you can get done, and with less stress. But after this deal, I really started to see that, with the right team, your business can go to places that I had never dreamed of. When Gerry and I had our original deal, there was no plan to build it and flip it in a year. I would have been happy to turn it into cash flow positive and achieve a 20% growth rate and settle for that in the first year. Then the next year, we could have focused on increasing profitability. But the team we put together changed all of that.

Fortunately, Brent and Dennis already knew each other and had no problem working together. Brent came in, and he got right to work. It was the end of August, and we needed to get moving fast. After all, we were in Las Vegas. We hadn't made much money in the summer, and now we were going into the off season. It always drives me nuts when I talk to business owners that have companies that are primarily in the AC business, and maybe a little plumbing, and they barely squeeze through the summer making a little profit. Somehow, they think they're going to make it up in the off season. But that never happens! If you can't make money when there's demand, how are you going to make money when the demand isn't there? You're not! But here we were, going into the off season with not much cash in the bank.

The good news is that they were using ServiceTitan at ACLV and Priority before I even started talking to them. Unfortunately, it was set up terribly. I will talk more about that later, but for now, people must see ServiceTitan as a very large tool that can aid you in running your business. It is still your business, and it's designed to let you run your business. It has recommendations for how to have it set up, but if you set it up around bad business procedures, it's like using a wrench to pound a nail or using a pipe wrench to put the lug nuts on your wheels.

Brent had only used ServiceTitan once at a company for a week, and theirs wasn't set very well either. He didn't have a lot of background in how it should look, but it didn't bother him very much. We would get ServiceTitan rolling a lot better later, but for now, we had very little time, and we had to get this ship out to sea. Brent took one look at his iPad, spent five minutes scrolling through it, and he was ready for his first call. In just that first call, he went out and made a $17 thousand sale.

I had flown to Las Vegas to be there and help in between my ServiceTitan Zoom meetings. It was in the middle of the COVID epidemic. We had all been working from home. I remember Brent walking in with his sale and I was encouraged. That was when I learned about what true salespeople are like. They don't care much about how things are set up, or what products you're offering, or even what the price is. They just sell.

The more differentiation you can give them, and the better the price book is set up, will make it easier for them to sell. It will help increase your average ticket and increase your close rate, but a great sales-person can sell just about anything. Just knowing that Brent could sell like that let me take a breath. It let me get to a place where I could think about building out the price-book and fix the processes. In the meantime, I knew Brent could sell. He wouldn't have his highest sales months, and it wouldn't be his highest average ticket until he had some better tools, but his talent was so great that he could outsell most salespeople who had the best tools.

I stayed up that night building out the price book, desperately trying to get the equipment in there that was available in Vegas. Gerry had been working hard on a deal with the Daikin representatives to sell Daikin and Goodman. The only problem was that it wasn't in our price book. We hadn't armed Brent with updated prices. He was modifying prices in the field for the first couple of days. I was adding in items as quickly as I could. Then I was making pre-built estimate templates for him to show good, better, and best options.

If you are reading this and you have ServiceTitan, and you haven't set up estimate templates for your salespeople and technicians, please put this book down and go set them up. At the time I am writing this book, fewer than 20% of ServiceTitan users have them set up and are using them. They are one of the most powerful things available for selling. For something as simple as selling a capacitor, you can have multiple options pre-built. When your technician runs across a failed capacitor, instead of building an estimate for the customer, you can click a button for the template and have multiple options pre-built for you. The first option could be a standard capacitor, and the second could be the Turbo 200 with a five-year warranty and the third could have an extended warranty, or whatever you want. The fact is that if you give a homeowner options, it usually turns out that they will then have a higher average ticket.

If you don't have them pre-built, then the techs won't take the time to build the options, and they will offer one thing. Or if they do build options, they won't spend twenty minutes writing up good descriptions to help the homeowner understand what they are buying and what the value truly is.

ServiceTitan has the data to show that when people use estimate templates and you present them with multiple options, you will see an increase in revenue to the tune of about 10%. That is huge! But unfortunately, most people simply don't set them up. But if you set them up, when a salesperson is in the home, they should be able to spend as little time as possible clicking around on their iPad or tablet and as much time as possible talking to the buyer and presenting to make that sale.

Brent, Dennis, and the rest of the staff were fighting hard in the trenches to drive revenue and dig out of the hole we were in. The least I could do is try to give them as many weapons as possible. The good news is that the sales started quickly building up. A week or two after Brent arrived, we went into September and quickly realized that as amazing as that sounds, we were going to outsell our July numbers in September. July is almost always your biggest month in Las Vegas, but the sales were so strong in September that we were going to beat them. It was a breath of fresh air. It would give me another month with my team to prepare for the off season. I called in people from my Fresno operation to help work on the business processes.

The first person I called was John Baird. "This thing is rolling. We have to build the car while it's moving," I told him. "It's going to be tough, but I could really use the help."

John was less-than excited, but he had worked for

me for a couple of years and knew all our processes. I was working full time for ServiceTitan and simply couldn't do what needed to be done in Vegas. John came in and helped tremendously. Seeing the sales happening, I knew the investment of time from John and others would be worth it if they would just hang in there.

Chapter Five

THE FIRST BUILDING BLOCK — THE BUDGET

When getting this rocket off the ground, you need a bunch of systems coming together at the right time to make anything happen. The timing is critical, and I don't think most business owners understand that. Whenever your timing is off, you lose a ton of money. That's because your business is made up of leads coming in, a call center that books the leads, techs in trucks that run the leads, parts that get supplied for the jobs, and a back office that collects the money, records it, and handles all the administrative stuff.

Let's say that you are getting ready for growth, and you hire technicians, spend a load on marketing to get the leads coming in, staff up the call center, but you don't have enough trucks to put the techs in to run the leads. What happens? All that marketing that you spent and your labor costs all goes down the drain. Remember that your business will only grow as fast as the weakest link allows it to.

In a very slow growing company, this isn't that big of a problem. The reason is that you can always slightly adjust the marketing, add one more tech, and get one more truck in a pinch. In most of these cases, the tech is the hardest one to get. The owner ends up hopping back in a truck to try to make something happen. That's when I hear a bunch of garbage from them saying, "We are so busy, even I had to step into a truck again."

I admire anyone who puts down his or her pride and is willing to make anything happen. That shouldn't be a badge of honor in our industry. If you have more than six or seven techs in the field and you are an owner and you must hop in a truck, it's because you didn't plan properly, and your company is suffering because of it. You should be working on the business and the people in the field need you to be doing that, unless you have someone else who does that very well.

So, what's the answer to avoid the scenario of an owner having to jump into a truck? Budgeting. When done properly, budgets allow you to see into the future and know how many people you're going to need. They let you know how many trucks you'll need and when. You should be able to look at lead times as well and say, "If I need 12 techs in June and I have nine in December, and I know it will take me four months to find them, hire them, retrain them, and put them in the field, then I had better start the hiring process in February."

When you have multiple people on a team trying to achieve a goal, the budget becomes the roadmap. The budget shows what everyone needs to bring to the table. It also shows the net profit at the end of the year that you need to hit if you're going to be successful. In a well-tuned company, the budget is also the scoreboard. You can tell if you are ahead or behind where you expect to be for the year. Could you imagine playing a competitive basketball game and your income and the incomes of all your teammates and their families' livelihoods are on the line and you don't bother to check the scoreboard?

One thing I often hear is a company talking about other companies, with some owners spending hours on the phone trying to hear rumors about their local competitors. A lot of people use other companies as a proxy scoreboard and compare themselves to other companies to make themselves feel better. I don't like doing that and I try not to. Tommy Mello from A1 Garage told me, "Losers focus on winners, and winners focus on winning." He even has those words on a sign in his shop. I wholeheartedly agree with Tommy. We all need to focus on winning and not focus on winners. Ken Goodrich, the guy that turned around Goettl Air Conditioning & Plumbing and the relatively undisputed most successful air conditioning operator in Las Vegas, told me there were 1,700 AC companies on record in Las Vegas. I don't doubt him.

When I first went to Vegas, there were two large residential HVAC and Plumbing companies–Yes Air

Conditioning, which Ken Goodrich sold to ARS a long time ago, and Goettl, in which Ken has an ownership stake. People asked me, "Are you going in there to compete with Ken?" I rolled my eyes and answered, "No. I'm going in there to make some money and build a company."

No one really competes with anyone but themselves in a market like that. I calculated there is at least $1 billion in total residential HVAC revenue and probably another $350 million in residential plumbing revenue in Las Vegas. (If you want to know how we calculated the total market share of a given city, go to howarddeals. com and click on the acquisition guide. It has a step-by-step video.) Goettl is one of the biggest, and Ken told me it would do over $50 million in revenue in 2022. That represents just about 3.8% of the total market share. To be clear, there are 1,700 HVAC companies there and the biggest one has just 3.8% share of the market.

When you go into a market, with few exceptions, you usually aren't having to "steal" or take anything from anyone. There is almost always plenty to go around. That's why I say that you are usually competing against only yourself. Set your goals, build your budget around it, and drive forward.

I've looked at over 100 shops and consulted for many of them. I've seen all kinds of budgets, from fancy ones that are hard to understand with 200 tabs on a spreadsheet to simple ones with one tab that doesn't cover much. You'll find the budget we used to run our business at howarddeals.com. If you don't have one, feel free to duplicate ours, or just make one of your own. Another option is ServiceTitan, which offers a free resource called the contractor playbook at www.servicetitan.com/field-service-management. They provide helpful tips about things from incentive plans to budgeting and everything in between. If the link is too long, just search for ServiceTitan contractor Playbook in your search engine of choice.

If you're reading this book and you haven't created a budget yet, don't worry! I was once in your position. Over time, the need to create a budget is still there. In Las Vegas, I had to figure out how to build a budget that was more complicated than anything I had ever made and yet simplify it enough to make it easily understandable and clear so that I could disburse it to the team. The issue I had was that I knew Vegas had been underperforming for a long time and didn't have basic procedures in place. I also knew that the Brent Buckley factor, our star sales agent, was going to change the game. Normally, I don't want to do very complicated math to get a budget, but I wanted to build something realistic, and it was hard to predict what that would look like.

The whole point of budgeting and forecasting is to make it realistic. It's okay to stretch your team but make goals that are attainable. If a budget is built properly, it will show what's possible so you can get the buy-in. If your team doesn't buy in, though, then it loses its effectiveness. One of the easiest ways to lose the buy-in is to quickly throw one together, give it little thought, and roll it out to your team. Then, when the numbers seem impossible to hit, the team starts losing interest.

For this budget, I had almost no reliable numbers to build a budget. I had gotten used to building in seasonality to a linear growth rate, but in this case, I had a growth rate that was going to curve like a hockey stick and I wanted to build seasonality into it.

I ended up missing a flight out of Vegas because of high winds, so I checked myself into the MGM Grand Hotel. It was going into a weekend and COVID was in full force. Vegas wasn't exactly hopping with people. Since my wife had left to visit family, I holed up in my hotel room and got to work on the planning for the year.

I sat at a little desk with my laptop computer, a big yellow notepad and a pen and hashed it out. I would only leave to get food and then go back to the room. I remember when I finally figured out the equation, I would use to figure out the hockey stick growth pattern. I jumped for joy when I tested it, and it worked.

I called Gerry, my partner, right away and explained what I did. I was literally jumping up and down in my hotel room. Gerry was trying to be as nice as possible although it was hard for him to share my enthusiasm since he seemed to feel sorry for me that I was spending the weekend in a hotel working on this. It's true that math isn't my strongest suit, but when I figured that budget out, I was on top of the world. It didn't make any sense to anyone but me, but I loved every minute of it.

Once I had the growth rate figured out, the rest fell into place quickly.

Before I left the hotel, I had a full budget, with margins for each department, how many HVAC service techs we would need in any given month, how many installers, and how many plumbers. We also knew about how much we would have to spend on overhead and what our net profit would be for the following year.

It was only September 2021, but we forecasted out for the end of 2021 and all of 2022. It was magical. We had a clear path to $2 million profit, or EBITDA) (Earnings Before interest, Taxes, depreciation, and Amortization).

I took the budget to the team and laid it out the following week. Now we had a plan and a vision of what we could do. We had a long way to go, but we finally had something to rally around. It would be a huge turnaround for the company and one of the quickest turnarounds of all time.

It makes me smile to think about how stoked I was that we were on pace to do $2 million in profit that year if we hit that budget. I still laugh when I think about it. You see, there was only one problem—my math was absolutely dead wrong! It would have been right, given normal circumstances, but this team was far above "normal." You might think that would have been the end of it. But it was just the beginning, and we would end up pulling off something out of this world.

Building a Budget

If you already have developed a budget and live by it, please skip this section so you aren't bored to tears. You can jump to Chapter Six. But if you are just getting started on budgeting, here is a guide to creating one.

Start by determining the biggest drawback in your business. What is the main bottleneck? Is it getting techs? Getting trucks? Getting leads? Whatever it is, start there. If you think you can only get three more techs for next year, and you have six now, then start your budget around that. Look at how much revenue per tech you can support with that size company and make that your goal. For example, let's say each technician can produce $40,000 in completed revenue per month in the summer. That means if you will have nine techs, you can produce $360,000 of revenue in June just from technicians. You can do installers separately.

Next, look at how many jobs you need them to run to get them to that revenue. Check your average ticket. If your average ticket on service is $500 dollars, then that means that they need to complete 80 sold jobs per person to complete $40,000 in revenue. Then look at your conversion rate. That's the percentage of calls your tech goes on that they actually sell. If you don't have ServiceTitan and you don't know these numbers, it's ok to take your best estimate. That's much better than not doing this exercise at all. If your conversion rate in the field is 75%, then take 80 calls and divide that by 0.75

and you get 107 calls. That means each tech needs to run 107 calls to sell 80 jobs to hit $40,000 in revenue for the month.

Here's something to be careful about. I have people tell me, "I can run a lot more than that because I can have my techs run four calls a day, plus we work Saturdays in the summer. We can push it." That's fine, but remember, they will need time to complete work that they sell as well.

For example, if they sell a compressor and must go back to install it, they'll need time to do that.

Next, look at the actual phone calls it takes to generate those 107 jobs. That's your booking rate. If you have a call booking rate of 80% then you need to take 107 jobs and divide it by 0.80. You'll find that you need to make 134 calls so that you can book 107 of them, to sell 80 of them, to generate 40,000 in revenue per tech. Also, keep in mind, you're generating jobs for nine techs. You need to multiply that by nine, which means you actually need to make 1,206 phone calls per month to generate enough jobs to keep all of your people busy in June.

It's much more effective to go to your marketing agency with this than to say, "The call volume feels light, let's turn up the advertising."

Once you have the revenue figured out and how many calls you need to make to achieve it, look at your gross margin and multiply your revenue by your gross margin. To make this easy, we're only considering your service revenue. If your service revenue is at $450,000 and you know your gross margin is 50%, then simply multiply $450,000 by 0.50 to get $225,000 in gross profit. After that, the rest is relatively easy because now you just enter your fixed costs such as rent, utilities, etc., and subtract those from your gross profit to get your net profit. If you have this all broken down by month, you should be able to get a forecast of just how much profit you will do for the year, and you can have a target that you should be able to hit.

Chapter Six

BUILT TO IMPRESS—OR NOT

I mentioned earlier that Brent started selling even without having his price book set up well, and before we had good office procedures in place. Our office was still disorganized. On almost every job we sold, we had to make a lot of special phone calls to get equipment. Our warehouse was a mess, stacked to the ceiling with old AC units that were still good in the eyes of the old owner, and we would sell them one day. Sometimes a homeowner would want a scratch-and- dent unit, and we would make some money there. Some units had about five inches of dust on them because it hadn't sold and never would.

In the conference room, the conference table was most likely bought at a yard sale and the conference chairs were probably bought at a second-hand store. Almost none of the chairs matched and the ones that had wheels, had at least one that was broken. If you wanted to move it, you had to push it around like it had a barbed hook dragging into the carpet. There was a separate plastic folding table from a wholesale warehouse at the front of the conference room that had some electronics on it. If you're still having a hard time picturing what our conference room looked like, imagine the nicest boardroom you've ever seen in a movie and then think the opposite. That was the conference room. The internal processes in the back office weren't any better. We had job checkout lists filled with random things that weren't necessary, and the office wasn't checking them, anyway. The techs were filling them out on every call for no reason at all. Plus, they weren't being truthful because they knew no one was looking at them.

I had just set up the basics of the price-book and we were making some good sales when I convinced one of my Fresno salespeople to come out to Vegas. ServiceTitan wasn't set up nearly as well as it was in my Fresno office, but it had some duct systems, ac units, and other things available. The Vegas office didn't look as nice as the Fresno office and our procedures in Fresno were much better than what we had in Vegas, but I didn't think that would be a big deal for him. He got out there, took one look at the setup in the company, and wanted nothing to do with it. He had seen what a company could look like and wasn't going to spend any time at this place. We even gave him a lead, but he said, "Tom, I can't even run this." I got frustrated and Brent ended up running the lead instead.

I talked to the sales guy from my other office, and he told me about his concerns with the Vegas office. He ended up going back to Fresno within a couple of days. This experience did two things for me.

First, I noticed that there was a lot of employee turnover at ACLV. People came and went regularly. There was a core that stuck around, but it was basically a revolving door. The guy I brought out from Fresno was a good sales guy and I realized what was going to happen to every other good employee I brought in that door. They were going to think the same thing, and they were going to leave. In the past, I hated spending any money on the office space. I saw almost no value in it. Over the years, I started investing in it at my Fresno company because we had the extra cash, and the employees liked it. This experience changed all that. Investing in making your space look decent isn't about looking nice after you're successful. It's about investing in your business so you can become successful.

People want to work in a place that they can be proud of. They want to be a part of a team that they can go home and talk to their spouses about and not be embarrassed. That means that the first impression they get when they walk in the door will tell them whether they should work for your company. If you don't get this part figured out, the people that stay at your company will be the ones that can't get jobs somewhere else. You don't want that.

Second, this experience made me even more grateful for Brent. He took a chance on us. After his last deal fell through, he really could have gone anywhere else.

People were even offering him a higher equity stake than I could offer him. But fortunately for us, he saw the team, and he saw the potential and he stuck it out. In the end, it paid off for him, but at that time, you couldn't see the end from the beginning. It also made me see how good a salesperson he really is. He can sell in almost any situation. He is an anomaly.

After seeing this, Dennis, the General Manager, pushed pretty hard to get the place cleaned up. And Gerry will admit that he had the same mentality that I used to have. A lot of the stuff stacked in the warehouse was because Gerry wanted it there. As contractors, it's hard to see the cost of clutter and we think that stuff has value and all it does is take up space. We think that someday, someone will need that one part we kept, and we will be the only ones in town with that part. Truth be told, if someone needs that part and it's no longer in production, the tech in the field won't know that you have it anyway and will recommend a full system replacement. Plus, the system is probably twenty years old and needs to be replaced, anyway!

I talked to Gerry and got him to take a step back and let Dennis make the decisions. It was hard for Gerry to let go, as it is for any business owner, but when he did, things started to pick up.

We also were elbow deep on fixing processes. There was a lot to correct, and it was like trying to boil the ocean. Simple things like deactivating the cumbersome job arrival checklist that was slowing techs down was a quick fix. But there were much bigger and harder problems to overhaul. For instance, we had decided not to use ServiceTitan payments, a feature that lets you process credit cards in the field. Gerry had decided not to use ST payments because he could get a third of a percent cheaper on the credit card processing fees if he used a third-party service. I have seen tons of business owners do this and it's gut wrenching.

With ST Payments, when a tech completes a job, he enters the customer's credit card information into ServiceTitan. ServiceTitan then marks the job as paid, deposits the funds into the contractor's bank account, and sends the transaction to the accounting program that the contractor is using. If you don't use ST payments, the technician who gets the credit card has to either use a third-party app or call the office to process it. The office has to go into their credit card processor's app, find all the transactions and reconcile them, one by one, to make sure they made it to the bank and make sure the technician marked it as paid in ServiceTitan. Then they have to reconcile it with their accounting software. That's not all. They also have to go into every job in ServiceTitan that doesn't have a credit card transaction and call the customer to get a card to get them to pay, which is always fun. This leads to hundreds of hours of time in the office, and in this case, tens of thousands of dollars of bad debt per year. We were literally spending over $100,000 in office wages and bad debt expenses to save a third of a percent in credit card processing fees, which was a fraction of what we were losing.

Things like these drag us down while we're trying to grow. We were putting sales on the board, which is what everyone wanted to see. What you don't see is that if you have terrible back-office procedures with a good sales team, it's like strapping a load of bricks to the back of a rocket. If the rocket is strong enough, it will get off the ground, but why would you do that? Why not get rid of the bricks and have it fly even faster and higher than before? I can't tell you how many profitable companies I saw during my consulting days that were carrying a giant bag of bricks and didn't even know it. In our case, we knew it and we were dropping off bricks as fast as we could, but we were about to get a big boost that would change the trajectory of that rocket big time and we knew nothing about that yet. It would stretch our ability to adapt and change and force us to move even faster.

Chapter Seven

KEY CHANGES TO ALMOST EVERY BUSINESS I HAVE ACQUIRED

We already discussed the idiocy of credit card processing manually, or as I sometimes put it, "Don't step over dollars to pick up dimes." Manually entering maintenance agreements and not having them automated yet in ServiceTitan is just as dumb.

Spend the time to automate everything. In the short and long run, it will save you time. If you have twenty different maintenance agreements, it makes it cumbersome and hard to keep track of. Just simplify it. Remember that if something is too hard for you to understand, your customers won't understand it either. Break it down to a couple of options, three at the most. Follow the In-N-Out model. Then it's much easier to automate as well.

Don't burden your technicians with unnecessary forms to fill out. Only require things that you absolutely must have. Just because ServiceTitan allows you to make an indefinite number of forms doesn't mean you should. Make the ones that are mission critical and cut all the rest. This allows the techs to be more efficient in the field and with their time. Your techs will thank you, your profitability will increase, and the accuracy of the forms you fill out will get exponentially better.

General Junk and Clutter—No one is impressed by it!

You will never make money keeping motors on the shelf that are a year old. If your people don't know it's there, when they need one, they will just buy a new one, anyway. My test is this: if it has dust on it, it's been there too long. It's taking up space and sending a message to your whole company that it's ok to hoard stuff. Before long, your trucks will start to look like that. If you have this stuff at your shop, it will be very hard to get rid of it, but you have to rip off the band aid and throw it in the dumpster. Another option is to tell your friend, the other hoarder who owns an AC or plumbing shop, that you'll sell it all to him for a thousand bucks and let him come take it away to hoard at his shop. It could save you the labor of getting rid of it.

Terminate any unruly techs and staff. I don't care how important you think they are. Trust me on this one, you will be relieved after the fact. They are sending a message to everyone on your team that it's ok to do whatever it is they are doing. For anyone on the team,

I would ask myself this: would I hire this person today knowing what I know about them now? If the answer is no, they must go. They are taking up a spot that could be filled by someone you could work with.

Build a real budget. About 90% of the companies I go into don't have a budget that is worth even looking at. Most of the companies above $20 million in revenue have them, though. That is not a coincidence. If you don't have a realistic budget, build one, let everyone know about it and check it monthly with your team and see if you need to reevaluate it. Don't just build it and leave it on the shelf. I know I'm repeating myself here, but building a realistic budget will be one of the most important things you do. (Refer back to Chapter Five which deals with budgeting)

Chapter Eight

THE BIG OPPORTUNITY

After we got off to a good start in September, we rolled right into October with the same sales success. I was blown away by what the team was pulling off. They were crushing the budget. The fixed expenses were in line with what we had expected, but the team was far exceeding the expected revenue, and they held the gross margin percentages in line with expectations. This led to a much higher than normal net profit.

To get down to the real numbers, in September, our budget was only $446,000. Let me put that into context. In July the actual revenue was $415,000. We projected to do more in September in Las Vegas than we had done in July. We weren't sandbagging this. We really put up a big number on that budget. The team came back and delivered $528,000 in revenue. I was amazed. Then in October we had budgeted $427,000, and they ended up doing $589,000 in revenue.

The gross margin was hovering a little above 40% and the net margin was coming in well above 13% in the off season, which I was happy with.

People ask what we were doing to drive leads like that in the off season. We only had a couple of things going—Google paid ads and direct mail. We used Stochastic Marketing out of Brentwood, Missouri, for direct mail and sent out a lot of tune-up mailers. We hadn't started system replacement mailers yet. Finally, we put a lot into outbound calling to the existing database and Gerry set up a plan to connect the customer service reps to the customers. In the end, had Brent not been able to convert those tune-ups into sales, we wouldn't have had the revenue we did. We prioritized the tune-ups and gave him as many of the 10+ year old units that we could, but we couldn't make that happen all the time.

I want to be clear here. Brent was almost exclusively acting as a tech running tune-up calls and very few demand service calls. He wasn't getting flipped leads as a comfort advisor yet because we didn't start that until January. But the guy was outselling most people I know, and he didn't even have sales leads. It was unbelievable. He did $402,000 in sales in September and $535,000 in October. Not all of it got installed in those months, which is why his sales were almost as high as the company's entire revenue in October. It was getting kind of scary. I actually thought about taking out a key man life insurance policy on him.

About mid-October, we got word through the normal technician gossip channel that a company called Climate Control Experts was having problems. I knew Collin and Trevor, the owners of the company that had acquired Climate Control a year and a half prior to that. Their company was the Flint Group, which had multiple holdings in its portfolio, but Climate Control was the only one that was having trouble. I did and still do, look up to Collin and Trevor. Climate Control Experts had more revenue than we did. We didn't know exactly how much, but it was about $6 million in revenue, where our firms, Priority Services and ACLV, had only about $5 million in revenue combined.

Since Gerry, Dennis, Brent and I were all friends, we didn't have a written agreement, only a bunch of handshakes. We had filed for a corporation in Nevada which, during COVID, took way longer than it should have. We were also applying for a new license, and we were trying to create a new company, but until then, we were operating under Gerry's company and Gerry owned it all. This was all done on trust. Even Brent and Dennis were working on a handshake. I will always look back and be grateful to those people who can make business deals on trust so they can move faster, because I know they will always live up to their word. Brent, Dennis and Gerry were those kinds of guys.

I really wanted Climate Control Experts because I knew that if I could get that company, strip out its excess costs and get their leads in front of Brent Buckley, we would have a truly profitable company. I had a couple of problems, though. First, I didn't have any money and people usually want money in return for their businesses. I found that out because I had a business partner at Lee's Air in Fresno that I had bought out a year prior and had to give him what I had, plus take out a large bank loan to fund the rest. I was just coming out of that when this came up. Second, since our paperwork was tied up, I didn't even have a company to do a merger. What I had was a strong desire to get the company. I reached out to the owners several times to talk to them about it. They told me they were fine, that they didn't need to sell it, and that they would turn it around.

Then a couple of their employees quit and came to us. The people at ACLV that hired them didn't know I was trying to buy Climate Control Experts (CCE). And I didn't know that CCE needed them to quit because their overhead was out of control and the employees that came over were overhead expenses. They let me know, though, that things weren't good.

Time went on and our October numbers were almost complete. We were going to show a healthy profit in the middle of the off season for the second month in a row, and I was jumping for joy. I decided to do something slightly dumb. I took out a piece of paper and wrote: "Tom Buys Ugly Houses Fast in Las Vegas" and then put my phone number after it. Then I crossed out houses and wrote above it, AC Businesses. Then, on October 30th,

I sent it to the guys at Flint Group and said that I was going to staple them to telephone poles in Vegas next week and I thought you should know.

They weren't impressed. In fact, they didn't even respond. But it started a conversation in the next couple of weeks and that got the ball rolling. They initially sent me information on their company that showed their profit for the year was only $240,000. This was a bummer for me, because if it showed a profit, then they would want money to buy it, and I still didn't have much.

I put together a plan anyway, even though I thought it had very little chance of success. I took my budget, showing us on a path to hit over $2.4 million in EBITDA by the end of 2022. Keep in mind, this was November 2021, and we hadn't even gotten to 2022 yet. My budget only started in September 2021, and we had beaten the budget for two months in a row. That's right. My plan was based on a two-month performance. But that was all I had. I was going to use it.

I had something else, though. I had worked with Collin in the past. He had told me about the rest of his portfolio, and it was impressive. The growth rate was solid, and this Vegas operation looked like a pain in his side. We had wanted to work together for a while, and this might be the opportunity to take the thorn out of his side, letting him focus on companies that were making him money. The others were also larger, making them more worthy of his time. If you can increase a $20 million revenue company by 20%, that's $4 million. Increasing

CCE by 20% would be around $1.2 million, which meant the return on his time wasn't as good in Vegas as it was with his other companies.

After talking to them, I also found out they knew how to fix it but neither partner wanted to do the work. Trevor was flying all over running companies, as was Collin. They would have had to go to Vegas for a couple months and dial it in, but that wasn't in the cards. I tried to appeal to them and show how my team could fix it so they could stop worrying about it.

I set up a Zoom meeting to show them my plan. I had even modified my forecast to show what the company would look like if we merged all three companies together. I showed my ideas about what the expenses would look like if we could trim down both sides. I showed on my spreadsheet how much more profit we would make. Of course, none of it had actually happened yet. They would have to believe me.

Then I dropped the bomb. We would do this, and they would get 10% of the whole company. Let's be clear, my grand plan was to take the two shops I kind-of had that generated $5 million in revenue and merge it with their shop that had $6 million in revenue and give them 10% in exchange. It was a really low offer, but I didn't have a lot more equity to give up because I had to spread it around for Gerry, Dennis, Brent and myself.

As expected, Collin and Trevor pushed back on my ten percent number.

"I have a really profitable company, and CCE isn't. I'm basing this off profit and not revenue," I said.

"You mean future profit," Collin quickly interjected. "You'll have profit in the future, but you don't have much now."

He was right, of course. It was a giant gaping hole in my pitch, but when you go to battle and all you have are chopsticks, you try to make them look like swords. You work with what you have, because that's all you've got.

Then they did something that shocked me. They said, "Okay, let's do it."

I couldn't believe we had a deal. They said they would have their lawyers draw things up. It was all going forward. I was blown away. Then a couple of weeks later, Collin and I were talking when I mentioned the $240,000 profit. I said that I figured he would have wanted a million bucks for a company like that and I asked why he gave up so fast. He looked at me kind of oddly, and said, "What do you mean $240,000 profit!? We had a $240,000 loss. Didn't you see that dash – in front of the $240,000? That's a minus symbol showing a negative profit." I thought that the dash was a bullet point. I really just missed it.

I pretended I already knew that, but that was a huge oversight on my part. Collin saw right through my act and started laughing hysterically. I had made the deal, and that was on me. I still wanted the deal anyway, only it wasn't the steal I thought it was anymore.

He looked at me and said, "It happens. I missed a zero once and made an idiot of myself when I thought something said 400,000, but it really said 4 million. Probably shouldn't do that again, though." All I could do was laugh at myself. Shortly after realizing that I had made a miscalculation, I did something that would take the most audacity that I had ever mustered. I noted that Collin and Trevor had about 500,000 dollars in the operating account at Climate Control Experts. I thought a lot about the losses we could potentially take on and the amount of rebranding and advertising that would need to happen in order for us to make money. With this all-in mind, I called Trevor and Collin back. I presented my proposal. I can't remember exactly how the call went, but I basically said something to the effect of "Hey guys, after we acquire the company, could you leave the cash in the company for me to build the company and I pay you back in 6 months? Also, could you give me that money interest free?"

They were basically in a state of shock. They said ok; you want our entire company for no cash in return and you also want us to give you 500,000 dollars as well? Does this mean we are paying you to buy our company? I told them no; it would be a loan and I would pay them back by May. I just couldn't give them interest, though. They almost laughed. They asked whether I actually thought I could make enough money selling air conditioners in 70-degree weather in March in Las Vegas to make 500,000 dollars or more in profit to pay them. The truth was that

I had a hard time believing that I could, but I told them, with absolute confidence in my voice, that I would. They were bewildered and dismayed, but they agreed to it.

I couldn't believe it. This would give me plenty of cash to get through a rebrand and get all new wraps on all my trucks and put our company on the next level. I just needed a way to make money in the off-season at an air conditioning company. That was going to be tough.

The deal is the easy part. It's integrating the companies and making money that's hard.

Chapter Nine

MARKET SHARE CALCULATION

How do you find the market share for whatever product or service you plan to offer in a community? To find the market of a given population for an air conditioning company, start with the number of residents. For the sake of round numbers, let's say your city has a population of one million. We then want to know how many households are in that area. You can look up the average people per household online for your area, but in most areas it's around 2.3 people per household. Take 1,000,000 and divide it by 2.3 to get 434,782 households.

Then you have to make some assumptions about how many of them you actually want to service. If you're an HVAC company that doesn't service apartments, but you live in a hot area, everyone has an AC unit. You may want to only service 66% of the households in your area. Take 434,782 and multiply that by 0.66 to get 286,956 homes that you actually want to service in your area. If you live in an area where the climate isn't as hot, half the homes may not have an AC unit, then that is something to consider as well. For this exercise, we will stick with what we have.

Next, we look at how often homes in your area change their AC unit. In a hot climate that isn't near the coast, I would estimate that they have them replaced every seventeen years. If they are near the coast with saltwater ruining coils, you may want to decrease those years. For this case, I would take 286,956 and divide it by17 to show that they replace about 16,879 units per year. If you are in an area where a lot of people have more than one unit in their home, you may want to take that into account too.

Next, I would take that 16,879-unit number and multiply it by the average price you charge to replace a unit. If your average ticket on installations is $20,000, then you would take 16,879 times 20,000 and find the total replacement market could be $337,580,000 in your city.

Most companies have found that brands typically don't get past 25% market share in a large city. There's too much competition. I would take that number and multiply it by 0.25 to get $84,395,000 as the total you could max out at for installs in your market under these conditions. Keep in mind, to get to 100% market share, you would have to receive 100% of the calls from every failed AC system, then have a 100% booking rate and a 100% close rate in the field to get to 100%. It simply isn't realistic in larger markets. If you live in a very small town and there isn't another AC company for 200 miles, then you may get close to that 100% market share number. For example, Trey McWilliams has an AC company in the middle of nowhere, Texas and has around 70% market share at his main location. I had to fly into Dallas and then drive for three hours to get to his shop. To add to your service department, I simply looked at my service revenue as a percentage of what my install revenue is. If my service revenue is 25% of my install revenue, I would take $84,395,000 and multiply it by 0.25 and get $21,098,750 as my maximum residential service revenue in that area.

Adding in plumbing is extremely difficult, for several reasons. If your area has a ton of houses that are 40 years old with clay sewer mains that are breaking daily, your plumbing revenue could be much higher than a plumber living in a city that has all schedule 80 sewer mains or cast iron. Then you must consider whether you do re-pipes and how old homes are in your area. You also have to determine whether they have copper, galvanized steel, or pex (a high- temperature flexible polymer pipe). Each municipality has a different code for plumbing. I've found most companies that have been strong on plumbing for a long time, don't push plumbing much past 30-35% of what their HVAC revenue does. It's a rough guess, but Ken Goodrich mentioned the exact same number to me. If enough people believe it, it must be true, right?

Chapter Ten

LOOSE LIPS SINK SHIPS— AND DEALS

Just thinking about this chapter makes me angry. This section is embarrassing and a total failure on my part and on the part of my team. I honestly don't even want to write about it, but there are critical lessons that I learned during this process that I feel everyone could benefit from. The reality is that even when you win great wars; you lose some battles and some of them are ones you would rather not talk about. But that's when we fail to learn.

We get on stage and talk about how we won the war, and everyone sits around thinking how great you are. Then, when that person in the audience has shortcomings of their own, they feel alone, and will never win a great war because they have failures. Too many times, we don't highlight the losses while on a podcast or on stage. It seems everything went smoothly, and everyone rode off into the sunset, but that couldn't be farther from the truth.

By late November, we had the deal worked out between Climate Control Experts and we were heading for a close date. We were in the due diligence period. We were putting all the pieces in place to make things as smooth as possible. This is always difficult because not everyone is aware of what is happening. You can't tell the employees until the deal is closing because you don't want the employees to get scared and start worrying about the unknown. Plus, if you tell them early and the deal doesn't close, then the employees will have gone through a roller coaster of emotions that wasn't necessary. You also don't want any surprises, such as uncovering lawsuits that happened in the past. You also don't want to say or do anything that will anger the other party.

Whether you're buying a business or selling one, after listing the business for sale, when a buyer decides they would like to purchase it, they usually send a letter of intent. This outlines how much the buyer is willing to pay and the basic terms of the deal. The time between the day the letter of intent is signed and the day the deal closes is when the deal is most at risk. It is the diligence period. It gives the buyer time to dig in and look through all the financials in a deeper way. They can verify all the things that were said during the initial offer.

A slight wrong turn or mishap during the diligence period could blow the whole deal. With this deal, Collin and I were friends. We trusted each other, and for that reason, we could move faster than usual. In business, the more trust you can have, the easier things always run.

When people think of business deals, they usually think of two people sitting at a table with their poker faces on. Both are looking at how to screw the other one. Their eyes are half squinted, thinking about what the other person must be thinking. They calculate their next move slyly. They sit there doing nasty, hardline negotiations like out of a scene from the classic movie The Godfather. Then, when they finally agree, they shake hands, and both walk away to meet their attorneys to write up everything to make sure that the other guy can't screw them.

In my experience, I've found that the best deals never work this way. This is especially true in the services industry, where families are involved. They built a business and kept it in the family for years and they are emotionally tied to the deal. The business is like their baby. They aren't going to do some hardline negotiation, splitting hairs over every penny, negotiating with 20 buyers to see who gets their baby. Usually, the deal is going to get done with the team that they feel like will help them the most, treat their employees the best, and take care of their long-term interests. Sure, money is a factor, but it usually isn't even the biggest factor.

I know of someone who was offered $40 million for their business, and they rejected it for an offer of about $34 million because of who the buyer was. The interesting thing is that in the end, the deal was a great one. The seller ended up making more money because he kept some equity in the company. The employees stuck around because they liked the buyer, and they had some equity as well. The business grew, and they made tens of millions more in the end. Nice guys finish first sometimes.

With the CCE deal, Collin and Trevor were not emotionally tied to the deal, but it took a whole lot of trust. They had to trust that our team could turn it around and make them money in the end. After all, they were giving up almost all the company. They were, after all, giving up all control, hoping things would turn around. I had to show them they could trust me, and I didn't want to cause them to have any question about that, especially in the diligence period when they could easily pull the plug on the whole deal.

Things were going well. We had a lot of partners by this point. Dan Antonelli had been brought in as a partner to help with all the marketing. I'll talk more about the market disruption he did with our marketing plan later. He really made things happen on that side of it. Then we had Brent, Dennis, Gerry, and me. All of us had to be aware of what was going on. After all, most of us were going to be diluted to give shares to the Flint Group. Then, as we got nearer to the closing date, we had to tell the person in charge of finance and the person in charge of all the staffing for installs and service, etc. We brought them in and let them know of the seriousness of the situation, and that if word got out, we would lose the whole deal and it would cost us millions.

We could have held off longer on telling all those people. I could have worked the deal myself, gotten it almost all the way across the line, and put a clause in the deal that said if the shareholders did not approve it, the deal would be rescinded. I knew I would have had the votes of the shareholders. It wouldn't have mattered. It just would appear a little slimy on my part, but it would have been less risky. Also, I could have just not told the other two employees until the last day. They were working on projects that would be transformed by this deal, and I didn't want them to be doing things that would have been irrelevant in a couple weeks. I tried to spare them the heartache.

I was at the office one day in November and one of the techs approached me about the CCE deal. This was horrifying. I kept a straight face and avoided the question, but I was reeling inside. I wanted to throw up. This was such a delicate deal, and someone had told a technician. I was shocked! This was on a need-to-know basis and the techs definitely didn't need to know.

To prevent any further leaks, I pulled the ownership and two office people aside and talked to them again about the necessity of confidentiality and how we had been extremely compromised by letting other staff know. At some point, the word was definitely going to get back to CCE, and it was going to be ugly.

I was frustrated. We made a deal that would benefit everyone and since we had some immature people on the team that couldn't keep their mouths under control, we could lose it all. To this day, I don't know who leaked it, or if multiple people did. I really don't even want to know. The only thing that mattered at that point was getting the deal across the finish line. We did all the damage control we could, but I knew it wouldn't be enough. I let Collin know what had happened, and he was frustrated too, but I didn't want him to get blindsided by it. This deal was based on trust, and I didn't want him to think that I was keeping something from him. He basically told me how stupid I was for trusting the people that I did, but the good news was that the deal was still on.

Fast forward about two weeks and I had to go to a ServiceTitan meeting in Mexico. It was the beginning of December, and the deal was set to close at the end of the month. I got a call from Las Vegas, and it wasn't good. Employees at CCE all knew about the deal. They were hearing rumors, and it was obvious that they originated from our team. Some of their employees were reaching out to our employees and asking if they should jump ship. It was a nightmare coming true. I had to call Collin, and I really didn't want to. After all, he was in Washington state and almost never came down to Vegas. Maybe he wouldn't know. Maybe we could let this slide and just move forward with the deal.

The answer was simple: I had to call him. Always be open with your business partners. They may be angry, but let the chips fall where they may. If you don't, it will be worse in the future.

I called, and I have never heard Collin that mad in my life. His words were colorful, to say the least. I didn't have much to say in response. He had every right to be mad.

After that call, I was pretty sure that the deal was over. He sent me some texts telling me to stop talking to his employees at his company. He was referring to it as his company now and not ours.

I had to let things calm down and see what was going to happen. I was in Mexico, and they needed me there. I couldn't just leave. It was frustrating because there wasn't much I could do. I let my team know of the issue and that we were probably going to lose the deal.

Then Collin did something that would benefit us all, and I didn't see it coming. He called me and told me he was moving the deal up! He wanted it done now. Looking back, it was a great call, and a brilliant solution to a really nasty problem. Collin couldn't really call off the deal. He was losing $9,000 a day on CCE. He would have to do this deal or shut the company down and liquidate the assets. On the other hand, since the employees knew about it, we couldn't wait until the end of the month to make it happen. Nine-thousand dollars a day in losses could quickly turn into $20,000 a day in losses if we lost a bunch of field employees and couldn't generate revenue. The answer was simple; move the deal forward.

Collin made the call to the attorneys and told them

to move the deal up to that weekend. It was Friday, and he wanted it done over the weekend. He had people pulling paperwork and throwing things together. We wouldn't even have enough time to get all the shareholder agreements done, so he put the whole thing under my name and Flint's name. I had 90% of it. We would bring in the rest of the companies and the other shareholders under one umbrella in the next 30 days, but he accomplished his goal. The $9,000 a day in losses were now going to be my losses, and if I screwed up and had employees quitting, it would be my problem. It was a great move on his part.

Unfortunately, I was still in Mexico, and I couldn't fix the company's issues from there. If I was going to let the information leak to the CCE employees, I would have to deal with the consequences, not Collin. The attorneys sent me the paperwork via DocuSign. I signed it while standing in the sun, in-between two buildings in Mexico. It took seconds. It was done. Now I was losing more money per day than I ever had before, but it still felt good. I was confident that we could turn things around. I just had to get back to the States.

I hopped on a plane two days later and was on my way to LA. The airport was a mess. COVID was in full swing, and I had to take a COVID test before leaving. The airport was packed with people, with COVID paperwork, vaccine paperwork, and piles of luggage from canceled flights and rescheduled flights from the pandemic. All I could think about was getting home to my house in LA. I needed to regroup and get on a flight to Las Vegas.

While I was flying home, Collin videotaped himself talking to the employees, announcing the merger. He sent me the video file, and I sent it to my video editors in Armenia. We would have a clean announcement to put out over video. It would be ideal to do it in person, but Collin couldn't make it on that short of notice. He had other plans that he couldn't move, so he would make it work. The ball was rolling.

When I got to Los Angeles, I had a headache, and my nose started running. I wasn't sure what it was, but I had already had COVID once before and I had just taken a COVID test to come home from Mexico and it was negative. I wanted to put it out of my mind, but my symptoms got worse, and I had to get tested. Sure enough, at the financially worst possible time for me, I had COVID again! I couldn't leave LA and I was losing $9,000 per day in Vegas. My frustration hit an all-time high.

Why am I sharing this situation with you? So, you can benefit from my hard-learned lesson. This all could have been avoided if we had just kept our mouths shut and let the deal happen on normal terms. I learned I don't care how much you trust people or how excited you are about an upcoming deal, and you want to tell someone about it—don't do it. The farther that information spreads, the easier it is to let it get out of control. Put your pride aside. Your friends will find out soon enough and even if they never do, it doesn't matter. What is more important? Being successful in your business or having other people who usually have nothing to do with your business, thinking you are successful in business?

The reality is what other people think does not matter. Until the time is right, keep your mouth shut, your head down, and work on your business. Wait to talk about it until after the deal is done, or you may be laying on your back one day, hit with Covid, while you lose $9,000 a day.

Luckily, my fever subsided quickly. I waited the required number of days before I could hop on a plane and get to Las Vegas. In the interim, my team had gotten to work. They went over and started work on merging the companies.

I wrote earlier that moving the deal ahead would work out for all of us, and fortunately, it did. Since everyone knew about the deal now, we could start working openly. Instead of waiting until the first of the year to start the merger, we had multiple weeks of a head start. We got ServiceTitan started on migrating the data into one ServiceTitan account. We were interviewing employees and making strategic hiring and firing decisions.

In the end, we would be profitable in January, but I don't think we would have if we didn't have that head start in December. We are all very lucky that Collin and Trevor didn't pull the plug on the whole thing when they had the chance.

Another example related to the theme of this chapter—watch who you tell about impending deals or even how public you are with your meetings. We would lose another deal, months later, because an employee saw me meeting with another business owner in a public place. That employee spoke to employees at other companies and speculated that we were looking to buy that company. I was totally exasperated by what happened because of that. I felt terrible for the other business owner who put his trust in me, and I assured him I wouldn't talk to anyone about it, and I had not. But I was embarrassed by what had happened. He was hurt. We must take these potential deals seriously. We shouldn't even need non-disclosure agreements in our industry, but we do because some people can't help themselves from talking. They want to talk and some of them even want to spread rumors faster than a bunch of high school kids. I have seen $100 million plus business owners get too excited and talk about things that they shouldn't be revealing. It's all about pride and immaturity. We need to focus on things that matter and honor our words. Don't make the same mistake that I did. It's true—loose lips really do sink ships.

Chapter Eleven

FIRST MONTH BLUES

From my experience, I have found that almost nothing goes smoothly in the first month when merging two companies together. I talk to a lot of business owners, and they want to know how to make everything go smoothly. Mergers are always at least a little messy, but you can look forward to things going better after you get that first month out of the way. If you are going to have to terminate some employment agreements, then they should be done by that time. You should also have the accounting and payroll all merged by then. The best part of having that month out of the way is that you can get your first profit-and-loss statement. You finally get to see whether the estimates you built into your budget were accurate. They almost never are 100% correct, but you get to see how far off you were, and you can rework your forecast.

If I had to give any advice to offer you about what to do during that first month, it would be to expect pain, and to rip the band aid off as fast as possible. I'll start with the hardest part and that's the terminations. Usually when you are merging, part of the reason for the merger is that you will reduce overhead because you have duplicate positions. People generally see these terminations as cold, and they will call you heartless. They may even tell you that you are a terrible person and that you only care about profits. However, they don't see the bigger picture.

In this case, if the merger didn't happen, everyone in that company would have lost their jobs, not just some of them. Unfortunately, someone or in our case, some people, have to be the bad guys that come in and make the decision about which people should stay and which people should go.

I have been through other mergers where the company wasn't in peril and the merger was done just for profitability. In that case, you, as a business owner, may feel guilty terminating positions to improve the profitability. To those owners, I would say this: there may be reasons to keep people for the long term even if it may not be in the best interest of short-term profitability. I understand that. Someone may have special skills or qualities that you will need as you grow. Other than those circumstances, you shouldn't feel guilty for making decisions that are in the best interest of your company as a whole, even when it affects people's employment. You have a moral obligation to act in the best interest of all the employees and not just some of them. You need to make sure that your company can be as strong as possible because you don't know when the next recession is going to hit. You don't know when the next wave or obstacle is going to happen that could cripple your business. The stronger and healthier it is, the more likely your company is to make it through those challenging times and continue to provide jobs to the area and services to your customers.

Always remember the reasons you had for going out on your own and creating or buying the company that you own. You went out because you wanted something better. You wanted something bigger or more interesting than you already had. If you do not create a company that is growing, the people in your company won't have the opportunity to grow as well. You will be denying them the same things that you sought when you went out on your own. If you don't focus on growing your company and doing what you have to do in order to make it grow, then the ambitious employees will probably leave, and you will be left with those who are less driven. The more motivated employees will leave to work with those companies that are growing, or they may go out and start their own company and become your competitor.

For that reason, I don't apologize for making the tough decisions. Nor do I blame the General Managers for doing what they need to do.

As for those employees who are terminated, they too deserve to be in a place that is growing. They will have the opportunity to go out and find new places where their skill sets can be used, and they can feel challenged and needed. Look at it this way. If you don't terminate them, they will be stuck in a spot where they are duplicating the work of someone else. Progress in their careers will be slowed, and it will be because the person tasked with guiding the ship, and who is being compensated for doing that guidance, was asleep at the wheel.

In this case, we had around a dozen positions that would no longer be needed. I brought in some people from Fresno to help with the process. They worked for me at Lee's Air. I had a couple of them conduct interviews and give me their recommendations. I already had a list of how many people we should need, but I needed to know which ones should stay to fill those spots. I went and interviewed some of the staff as well for certain positions, such as finance, that I felt needed my input.

After getting all the feedback, we had to turn it all over to the general manager, who had to make the final call on each of them. I mentioned this earlier, but this point is critical. If you have a general manager, it is always vital to empower them to make their own decisions and for you to trust their decisions. If you don't do that, then they won't feel any ownership over the decisions that they made. You should have a bonus program in place based on profitability. But if they don't feel they are driving the ship and that they can affect profitability, then the bonus incentive won't be useful. It won't drive them to perform. They will just feel like they are filling a seat on the bus. They won't stick around and work extra hard and go the extra mile to make things happen.

I could tell that it was tough for Dennis, our general manager. I could see the look on his face, knowing that he would have to let some of his employees go. He had personal relationships with many of them. No matter how many terminations you have done in your life, it never gets easy. You must just push through it and get it over with.

Dennis made the final calls. I agreed with most of them and didn't agree with some others, but that doesn't matter. At the end of the day, we gave our feedback, but he had to make the choices.

Some business owners are tempted to take this a little slower and lay off a couple of people at a time over several months. They feel like it won't hurt the culture as much. But if you're an employee and you see people being terminated once every few weeks for months and months, all you can think about is whether you'll be next and that can actually destroy culture. Accept the probability that your culture is going to take a hit when you lay people off right after a merger. But if you rip off the band-aid, the pain can leave quickly, and the culture can get back on track.

After a merger, you need to get to profitability as soon as possible. Fancy office furniture and employee barbeques help culture, but they will never compensate for losing money. The best thing for culture is being a winning team. You may say, "No one in my office knows if we are winning or losing, because I don't show them the profits." If that's the case, I would hate to work for you because no one wants to play a game and not know the score. The score for each position might be different. For the Customer Service Representative (CSR), it may not be the net profit of the company, it may be their total booked revenue or their call booking rate, but they need to see the score, none-the-less.

If you don't show them the score, you won't get ambitious people. You will get people who just want to punch a clock. That will probably be the same person who posts on Facebook about how he or she can't get employees motivated and how they don't think like a business owner. If you think that just because you don't show them the score, that they won't know if they're winning or not, you're just kidding yourself. Every employee knows how to see the look on his or her boss' face to see if the boss is stressed. They can all feel the attitudes and demeanors of the leadership. So, I'll say it again, the best thing for culture is winning, period. Employee get-togethers are just icing on the cake, but you need cake first, and that comes with winning.

People ask me about severance packages and whether we use them. We use them on a case-by-case basis. In some cases, a promise or expectation of long-term employment was implied, and you may feel obligated to give someone a severance package to help them on their way. In other cases, you may have a key role that needs to be transitioned slowly, but you need to let the employee know they are transitioning and that they will no longer have a job in the long term. In that case, a severance is more of a compensation for working with you during that transition period.

While terminations were being figured out, we had to get all payroll migrated. With the employees, this can be touchy. There's nothing worse than an employee feeling like the new boss is going to screw them over. I handled this by giving a presentation to the team and being very open about wages. It went like this: "No one is taking a pay cut. We're looking at everyone's benefits and making sure everyone is getting comparable or better benefits, and we will have this all sorted out in the next week. Any questions?"

The worst thing you can do in this situation is not say anything at all. If you don't give them the information they are looking for, they will get it from each other or their imagination. Be open and communicate as much as possible.

Accounting can also be tough. I found it useful to hire a consultant to do some of the work to migrate everything together and then turn it back over to our finance people. Almost all the employees who were going to be laid off were let go in December or early January. The payroll was migrated, and we lost very few field staff over payroll issues. The first stage of the accounting migration would be done by the end of January. We completed profit-and-loss statements by February 10th. The early transition was relatively quick and once we got through it, people could feel more secure and start working on what was needed, which was turning a company around in the middle of the off season in Las Vegas. We had a decent amount of cash in the bank since Flint group loaned it to us, but we couldn't afford to burn through it. It's an understatement that selling air conditioning in Vegas in February is tough, but we would have to figure out how to pull it off. It would be no easy task.

Chapter Twelve

ONE TEAM - ONE BRAND

When putting this whole deal together, we didn't really know how it would all look in the end. I had no idea we would be able to buy Climate Control Experts. We could have moved forward with just the first two companies, Priority Plumbing and ACLV. I knew we would need a rebrand, though. Early on, we started working with Dan Antonelli from KickCharge Creative.

If you don't know who Dan is, his New Jersey-based company, KickCharge Creative, does the branding for most of the major players in the plumbing, air conditioning, and electrical industries. His designs are not traditional. He and his team make brands that work. They develop incredible logos and truck wraps and help you with brand stories that actually get noticed, and we definitely needed to get noticed.

I don't want to spend too much time talking about branding because there are literally entire books written on this subject. In fact, Dan Antonelli wrote a book called *Branded Not Blanded,* and I highly recommend it if you're looking for more information on branding. I will, however, go into the specific issues we faced.

The problem we had was that with the latest merger, we now had three brands. Many people, when they buy a competitor in the area, think about running their brands independently. They usually give me some story about how they'll lose their customers or the customers of the company that they are acquiring if they rebrand it to their main brand or if they get a new brand all together. The truth is that I'm usually able to retain 85% of customers in a new acquisition when I tuck them into my brand. (I will discuss how we do that in a later chapter.)

There is a cost to running multiple brands under one roof. Your cost of marketing gets to be significantly higher than it needs to be. That's because you need to hit a customer multiple times before they start to recognize your brand. Studies show that it needs to happen seven to nine times in a month. Some say it now needs to be nine to twelve times because people are being hit with ads all day long every day. Whatever the number is, when it comes to brand recognition, your frequency matters a lot. Your billboard might be one spot where you hit them. Your Facebook ads might be another.

If you combine your brands, your marketing can go a lot farther in getting the frequency you need. If you have to run two sets of billboards and two sets of Facebook ads, you'll be cutting your frequency in half.

You also have to manage multiple sets of uniforms and truck wraps and everything else. I've tried it, and I am running into that problem at a company I own in Australia right now. Trust me, it's not fun. Running three brands was out of the question.

The next biggest issue with branding is recognition itself. Almost every air conditioning company has a logo with a red and blue circle around it or a snowflake and a sun or some variation, or red and blue or orange and blue, usually on a white van. The name of their company is usually the last name of whoever founded it or some other generic thing like Cool Now, or Fast AC. When they drive down the road, and a potential customer sees the truck driving past them, I can almost guarantee that no one remembers the brand unless they have already used you before. One more thing, never, ever, call yourself something like AC for Less, or Cost Less AC. Customers act like they want a deal all the time, and they do want it, but they also want to pay less for top quality service. People go to a nice steak house and love to get a deal when they are there. They love getting gift cards to go to a premium steak house, or maybe they know the owner and get a deal somehow. No one wants to go to a restaurant that looks or sounds cheap. If you don't believe me, try taking your spouse or significant other to a steakhouse called Cheap-o Steak. Places like that don't even exist because no one wants to go there. Don't market yourself as the low-price leader. You won't be able to make the profit you need to stay in business unless you can do extremely high amounts of volume, such as Walmart or Amazon, and you surely won't be able to pay your technicians or yourself the wages that they deserve.

If you own one of these companies or some version of what I mentioned, you are probably saying, "My customers tell me they see my trucks everywhere." That's great. But they're your customers, obviously they'll recognize your trucks. You need to stick out in the minds of people that have never done business with you, not your existing customers.

Back in the day, I had the red and blue logo at my company, Lee's Air. It was the last name of the founder who I bought it from, and when I did the rebrand, we kept the name even though I hated that idea. But we truly had a lot of brand recognition in the area, because I did my rebrand too late. Most of you don't have a lot of market share, even if you think you do. If you are worried about it, go to **howarddeals.com** to calculate your market potential before you do a rebrand.

Once I did the rebrand, we switched to this hideous green/brown color at Lee's with blue lettering. I hated it. But Dan loved it. He told me it would do well. We rebranded early in the year. Within months, people were saying, "Gosh, you guys were already big, you must have tripled in size! You are everywhere now."

I had not added a single truck, but now even people who knew who I was would see our trucks from a mile away. Before, they could barely see our white van in the distance.

Then the summer hit. We couldn't figure out what was going on. Every year, when we made our budget, we forecasted how many inbound calls we could expect based on our marketing budget. We would accurately estimate it to plus or minus 10%. From that, we would hire customer service representatives accordingly.

But that summer, our office was flooded with calls. We were losing 75% of our calls on some days. We ended up getting three times the inbound calls that we had expected. It was a nightmare on many levels. We had long-time customers that couldn't get through. All of our CSRs were working overtime. We were shutting down every marketing campaign we could, and we still couldn't stop the calls from flooding in. When it was all over, I had to sit back and think about what had happened, and I finally realized that all of our previous marketing simply had not been as effective as it could have been because it wasn't memorable. Now, with the same marketing spend, after a rebrand, it became much more effective.

So, if you are telling yourself that you really need to rebrand, but you haven't pulled the trigger, just get it over with. Don't tell yourself all the lies that I told myself about how you can't do it because you will lose customers.

At any rate, when I got to Vegas, I knew for sure that we needed a rebrand and we had to bring everything under one roof. I talked to Dan, and he had a great idea for a brand. He called it Fetch-a-Tech. It was a brand that could be used for all home services, but it was also clear that it was for technical stuff like AC, electrical, or plumbing. Besides that, there are a lot of things you can do with that name. The logo became a dog with a wrench in its mouth. There were all kinds of things we could put on the truck and on the website such as "Dog gone good service," or "Service that is a breed apart".

The greatest aspect of all this was that the brand could really stand out. I was so excited I took it to the team and Gerry, who handled the marketing. Right away, they could see Dan's genius in it. Gerry loved it and wanted to run with it; however, the rest of the team wasn't too excited. All they saw was a friendly dog on the side of the truck, a cartoon. The team looked at me, puzzled. One tech spoke up and said "Well, could you at least make the dog into a rottweiler or something? That would look cooler?" I asked Dan just to say that I did, and you could hear Dan's frustration. The answer was no.

Many people make the mistake of selecting a brand that they like. I have news for you; you aren't your customer. You need a brand that they're comfortable with. Studies show that women make up to eighty percent of the decisions for homes. Statistically, many of these women are homeowners, are above the age of thirtyfive, have some college education, and use the internet and online news sources regularly. Let's call your target customer Ms. Jones. She found you while searching Google and trusted you to send out a qualified technician to her house. She has never met you before or any of your technicians. Just like everyone who has ever read Consumer Reports, or seen an episode of the local news that did an investigation into contractors, she is probably a little apprehensive about getting ripped off. This is true regardless of whether the technician you send to her home is male or female. The last thing that the average Ms. Jones wants to see when your technician rolls up to her house is a dog on the side of your truck that looks like it could have been in a horror movie. You are trying to build trust here, not your ego. Just trust the process and you can get a logo that helps build trust with Ms. Jones.

On a side note, Ms. Jones is a residential homeowner. She probably doesn't use terms such as HVAC, Hydro Jetting, or Capacitor. Those are terms you may use in your company, but Mr. and Ms. Jones don't use those terms. If you want to market to them, leave those terms off the side of your truck and any other advertisements. If you are advertising to commercial building managers or someone like them, then it's a different story.

In the end, we decided to go with the brand as Dan had designed it. The problem was that when we made this decision, we were short on cash. Dennis was going to have to dump money like crazy to re-wrap all the trucks. We were going to have to spend a lot on a new website, new paper collateral, etc. I made a deal with Dan that we would give him one percent of the company to do all the branding and web design in exchange for him doing it for no cash. It would be a great deal for him in the future, but we didn't know that at the time, and I was determined to do this whole deal with no cash out of my pocket. I owned a successful business in California, but I wanted to prove that you could do this without any other resources. He agreed, and Fetch-a-Tech was born. We were off to the races. Well, kind of. It was December 2021, and the website wouldn't be done until March, but at least we had a vision. We were now prepared to migrate the accounting and the corporations into one. The process and paperwork on that is daunting, and you must know what you want to do and have a vision before you start that process.

For more information about branding, how we approach marketing on a smaller budget, market size calculations, and other marketing related articles about my companies visit **howarddeals.com**. Dan published a book called *Branded, not Blanded* that is pretty incredible. It goes into depth on what makes a great brand.

Chapter Thirteen

ACCOUNTING AND REPORTING, AND THE REST OF YOUR INSTRUMENT PANEL

After figuring out the branding, we couldn't wait to start making a profit. As I mentioned earlier, Brent could sell, regardless of the situation. Our back-office procedures and our branding and general execution would magnify what he and his sales team would do. We had to get stuff in order fast to pull in the large numbers we needed.

The biggest piece of the back-office that had to be handled first was accounting. It may not seem that important and it's nothing but adding numbers, but improper accounting, even if it's good enough to not bankrupt you, will slow down your company more than almost anything. It may involve an issue in your company that you're not even aware of. It leads to slower decision-making because managers no longer trust the numbers, over cautious owners become afraid to pull the trigger on acquisitions or bulk inventory orders to get better discounts. Meanwhile, managers who don't understand their books are afraid to give great incentives to employees that would have driven performance because they aren't confident they'll have the money to pay those incentives. These are symptoms of poor accounting and inhibit growth.

I equate proper accounting and reporting to the instrument panel in a plane or the dashboard in a car. Most of the small business owners I meet think accounting is there to allow you to pay taxes at the end of the year. In most cases, their profit-and-loss statement isn't even ready for viewing until tax time. They monitor their bank account closely because that's what they gauge the success of their business on. However, this is probably one of the worst ways to run a business. It's like flying a plane with no gauges. In your business, your cash position is your altitude, your inbound leads are a lot like the fuel in the tank, your sales are a lot like the throttle, and your profit margin percentage is a lot like your trajectory. If you don't have gauges, you can tell that you are flying and you have a rough idea of where you are, but if it gets cloudy, you may not know your altitude until it's too late. You can push on the throttle all you want and give it more gas (driving more sales), but if your trajectory (profit percentage) is pointed down toward the earth, you may be flying right into the ground or into a mountain and you would have no idea.

If you are in the residential air conditioning space, let's say you sell a job in August for $20,000. There is some duct work and an air conditioner in the contract. Your cost for the materials and equipment is $6,000. Then you have permits that are $200 and then commissions that are $2,000, and your labor on the job is $2,000 dollars. You pay for the permit and complete the job and collect $20,000 dollars from the customer on August 20th. You pay your labor and commissions on the next payroll, which comes two weeks later, in September. You pay your supplier for the equipment and materials on 45-day terms. You pay them at the beginning of October. If you're looking at your bank account on August 25th, it looks like you only had $200 in costs for the month and $20,000 in income. Then in September, you paid commissions and labor totaling $4,000 and you have no income. Then in October, you pay your supplier $6,000 and you have no income associated with that either. Bottom line is that you go from thinking that you are a business genius in August and probably taking a family vacation in September with all your extra funds, to a broke guy in October that probably can't pay his bills. This is a very simplified scenario, but it shows why you can't be running your accounting on what we call the cash system. You may want to pay your taxes on the cash basis and when you are a small business, you can make that choice. But you should always be viewing your financials, at least monthly on the accrual basis.

If you don't know what accrual is, let me explain quickly. Take the example above, but the difference would be that on your profit-and-loss statement in August, it would show that you generated $20,000 income, and that you had $10,200 dollars in expenses. The cash is mostly in the bank, except for the $200 dollars for permits you spent, but the rest of the costs are in "Accounts Payable." This will draw the cash down in the future. This also shows the expenses tied to the revenue that caused those expenses. Now, when you check your financials monthly, you can get an actual idea of what is happening in your business.

Large companies do not run on a cash basis. It simply is not workable. If you aren't running your business on the accrual method or you can't get your financials done in a timely manner yet, accounting is one of the easiest things in your company to outsource. There are hundreds of companies out there that can handle everything, and it's not that expensive. Make that move as soon as possible. Some of the people I have used to help me with this are Backyard Bookkeepers, Lynn Wise from Contractor in Charge, Meghan Likes from Likes Accounting, and Kathy Nielsen. These are ones that I have personally worked with but, if you are on ServiceTitan there is a list of ServiceTitan Certified Providers at https://www. servicetitan.com/certified-providers. There, you can find people that can help with things, including accounting that has demonstrated competency in handling the export process from ServiceTitan to your accounting software and how to manage your job costing and purchase orders in ServiceTitan.

When I walked into what is now Fetch-a-Tech, we

had just combined the three companies together and had to clean up accounting. Some people think sales drives everything, and I'll tell you that sales are absolutely and critically important, but they aren't everything. Among other things, you need to have your flight instruments ready, and our accounting department was a bit of a nightmare. Cash was being handed out arbitrarily to technicians and various other people as bonuses. The financials were not coming monthly, more like whenever the accountant got around to it, and with three companies combined, we had six people doing payroll, accounts receivable, accounts payable, and general accounting. We realistically only needed three at the most. In the end, we reduced the number to three people working on accounting and payroll, and they started rocking and rolling. The three ladies who worked there kept those financials accurate and up to date. They closed the books more accurately and faster than any company I've had so far. I like to get closed financials for the previous month by the 10th to the 15th of the following month. I don't even ask or expect to get them any faster. Jayne, who ran that department, was getting them to me by the 4th or 5th of the month. I was amazed at how well and how fast she made it all happen.

To me, accounting is the unsung hero of most companies. I can't tell you how hard it is to get an accounting department to provide you with accurate financials in a timely fashion. I've had dozens of accountants working on my books at various companies.

To find a good one is like finding a needle in a haystack and they can make an enormous difference in my company. Having a poor one is like flying an airplane and not being able to trust any of your gauges. Art, my former accountant in Fresno, is one of the good guys. He pulls strings behind the curtains at three of my California locations and keeps that plane flying. He is quiet and gets no credit for anything, but he makes it happen month after month. Jayne did the same at Fetch-a-Tech. We could make a lot of fast moves because I trusted Jayne's numbers.

For example, let's say that you want to do a bulk order on equipment to get a cheaper price, but you are not sure you're actually making money as fast as you thought you were. Are you willing to pull that trigger quickly? Are you willing to make an order that could bankrupt you if you owe more money than you thought and you actually need more cash than you thought?

The truth is that running a business isn't just like flying a regular commercial airliner. Commercial airliners fly a normal path on a predictable schedule. Some businesses try to run that way. You start at the beginning of the year, you take off, and you make some profit right on schedule. You make enough profit to get up to your expected altitude, you cruise for a while and then you spend some of that profit and come in for a landing around tax time.

A top-notch accounting team or controller, combined with a top-level operations person, a top-notch sales team and a great marketing person, can turn that commercial airliner into a fighter jet. It gives the operator or owner the opportunity to be a fighter pilot, that can bank right or left, dip or climb in altitude at a moment's notice. For instance, soon we would have multiple times where we offered large amounts of cash to buy up small companies in our area and one of them actually went through. We had to drop over a million dollars in cash, and I was able to decide in seconds because Jayne was running the books. I knew exactly where our cash balance was and what I could expect to drop in the coming months.

When I asked the Flint Group to leave $500,000 in the bank for us to use to do a rebrand and build the company, I knew I would spend it, but I also knew that Gerry had the marketing under control and Brent Buckley could drive the sales we needed. All we had to do was push on that throttle to get some sales made and we could pay the money back in time, even though it was the off season.

We had to make deals with manufacturers for better equipment pricing based on projected volumes, and later I would have to make forecasts to project what our final profit would be to tell the potential investors. All these things were possible because of a very reliable accounting team that gave me the numbers I needed in record time. It truly felt like I was flying a fighter, and I felt like we were pushing that plane to its limits, but Dennis and the team held the plane together and boy, did we fly.

Chapter Fourteen

POSTING WINS IN JANUARY

After acquiring Climate Control Experts (CCE) in December 2021, that was the last time CCE would take a loss. The newly formed Fetch-a-Tech would be profitable in January. We would post a $166,000 net profit for the month. The budget had called for a $40,000 net loss. That put us over $200,000 ahead of budget by the end of the first month of the year. We couldn't have been happier. That initial budget only showed a $2.5 million net profit for the year, but after the first month, I was afraid to get too excited, since we really only had one big win after CCE had been acquired. As I mentioned before, Jayne and her accounting team were on top of the numbers. We were getting them fast and knew exactly where we stood.

The problem was, we knew exactly where we stood when it came to inbound call volume as well, and where we were standing wasn't good. We knew that February and the coming months would be even lower because the weather would get even nicer in Vegas, and we had to do something. Gerry, who was now strictly focused on marketing, was going to put the pedal to the metal and drive as much as he could with basically no brand recognition whatsoever in our area.

We typically break marketing in the home services industry down into two types. We have brand recognition campaigns and direct-sale campaigns. Branding campaigns just let people know who you are. They include things such as billboards, radio commercials, television ads, Facebook ads, YouTube ads, etc. The intent of most of these, with a few exceptions, is to get people to recognize your company and get comfortable with it.

Direct-sale campaigns are different. In these campaigns, you have some type of call to action to get people to buy right away. These are usually direct mail campaigns, Google Pay-Per-Click campaigns, Google Local Service Ad campaigns, Yelp ads, Home Advisor ads, etc. In this case, people are going to a platform, looking for a service, and you are hoping to get the customer to pick you instead of someone else.

People that do marketing in our industry mess this up all the time. They miss the point of each type of media, and the effects are catastrophic. Let me explain why. I'm sure you have seen billboards for a plumbing company or AC company that say "$2,000 off a new AC unit, call now!" Or maybe you have heard a radio commercial for an AC company that says, "Free water heater with every new air conditioning system purchased." Think about it. Our industry, in most cases, is a necessary evil.

No one wants to buy an AC for fun. They might buy cars for fun, they buy boats for fun, but they don't buy a new air conditioner for fun. They only call you because they need you. They want their living situation to stay comfortable.

When someone driving down the road sees a billboard advertising $2,000 off a new AC unit, is that supposed to get them to call? Does anyone say "I have an extra $25,000 lying around and they have a deal going on right now, so I'll call them to get an AC unit. And I'll even pull off to the side of the highway right now to write down that phone number because that seems safe. Then I'll call them tonight, because I love spending money on air conditioning when mine is not broken!" NO!!! The only time that happens is in a delusional marketer's dreams. Trust me, I know, I used to be that delusional marketer. I speak from experience.

What really happens is Ms. Jones' AC unit fails on a Tuesday, and it's 100 degrees outside, and she is frustrated. She has little time to deal with it between work and family life, so she pulls out her phone and does a quick search on the internet and scrolls through a couple of listings to see who has a lot of reviews and looks legit. She would have recognized your company because she passed by your billboard thirty times, but it was jumbled with a bunch of garbage like a phone number and an offer that she can't read while driving down the freeway. That billboard pretty much just wasted your marketing dollars.

You have a decent number of reviews, so she calls you to come out. You go out and sell her a new air conditioning system and since your service is better than your marketing, you get it done quickly and get paid. Ms. Jones gets her new AC system, and her house is comfortable again.

Then, a week later, Ms. Jones is driving down the highway and now she has done business with your company. Now her brain picks up on your billboard. Behold! Ms. Jones notices your $2,000 off offer and she thinks, "I just paid full price for my AC unit!" Then you get a phone call from Ms. Jones, who wants $2,000 dollars back and you have to give it to her, or she is going to trash your reputation online. Congrats on the billboard. I must add one more thing. Please don't put your face on the billboard. No one wants or cares to see it. The only people that get away with that are people who have mascots for their brand that kind of look like them and make that part of their logo, such as Colonel Sanders from KFC or, years ago, Dave Thomas, founder of Wendy's. Ken Goodrich from Goettle pulls it off with the brand story of the boy holding the flashlight for his dad and Tommy Mello from A1 Garage door with the caricature of himself that kind of became his brand. Otherwise, no one wants to see your face on the billboard. It takes away from what you really want the customers to see and remember, which is your company. Tell people how great your company is, not how big your ego is.

Branding is there to boost the effectiveness of your

direct sale campaigns. The point of branding campaigns is to get customers to remember you and be comfortable with you. That way, when there's a problem and they do an internet search, and they see your name, they're more likely to click on it and book with you.

Ismael Valdez from Nexgen Heating and Air talks about it like this. We all have fishing boats, and we all have our nets in the water. The nets are our direct sale campaigns. We all try to position our boats in the best spots and try to get in front of the other boats and we try to make our nets as big as we can. That's all related to how we run our direct sale campaigns. Branding campaigns allow us to move the current in the water to push more fish into our nets. Some branding can be expensive and there are ways to really win with it, but you need to know what you're doing.

There are places where offering a deal may make sense. Let's say you have a Google ad that shows a deal for $2,000 off of a new AC unit. It takes you to a landing page that shows rebates for that amount from the local government or utility company or whatever you choose. This may get people to book with you instead of someone else.

In all of this, I speak candidly and bluntly about how ridiculous some of our marketing practices are. Some things are obviously outlandish after you step back and look at them from a different angle. The best thing you can do is look at your marketing from your customer's perspective. Ask your customers questions. Do not ask them if they like your ad. If they know you, they will always say "yes."

Talk to people who don't know you and list five companies in your area, including yours, and ask if they've ever heard of any of them. You may be surprised if they know any of them. Another thing you can do is go to a mall and ask people if they know any companies in your industry in your area. Then they can give you an unbiased answer. Many times, they'll know one or none. You'll quickly find out whose branding is working and whose isn't.

The next thing you can do is think about radio ads, billboards, etc. Think about any you remember. Have you ever written down a phone number, ever, from a radio ad, TV ad, or billboard ad? If you ever have, it must have been for something that was a huge deal and almost nothing that we offer in home services has that much of a hook.

Gerry had these lessons figured out. We give him a lot of credit for knowing everyone and helping set up these connections to people that made the Fetch-a-Tech deal happen, but he was also a pretty good marketer and made things happen in that regard. We started pushing out Direct Mail campaigns like crazy. I don't get paid or have any financial interest in Stochastic Marketing of any kind, but Mike Layton at Stochastic has been one of the few companies I've used that have produced good results for large direct mail blasts to prospects. Gerry worked with Mike to get mail pieces for Tune-ups that had a fantastic impact. Since we had such an awesome sales team, we knew if we could just get them in front of people, they would perform.

Gerry pushed Marketing Pro from ServiceTitan to its limits as well. Every customer that saw an estimate and didn't buy would automatically get an email with another offer trying to get them to close. Then there are all the automatic emails and post cards you can send out for holidays and other things. I get paid by ServiceTitan, but I can tell you, I use marketing pro at every one of my companies and it is a game changer. I pay full price for the product as well and I think it's one of the most valuable products ServiceTitan offers. It makes no sense to rig something to work using Zapier, or other products, to send it to a third-party platform just to save a few bucks on ServiceTitan. If we spent our time fiddling with that stuff, we would be half the size we are today.

We pushed heavily on Google, but beware of any system that is auction based. Google has been one of the most powerful tools in our industry, but you need to know what you're doing. You need to monitor your spending and your results. This goes for Google Local Service Ads and Pay Per Click campaigns. Do not be afraid to turn things off that aren't working. During our run at Fetch-a-Tech, we didn't have Service Titan's ads optimizer, but I would have killed for it back then. It's an add-on product that they have, and it checks how your ads are performing on Google and tells you what to turn up and what to turn down. They will even start looking at your capacity to turn ads down as your capacity fills up. It's awesome. We have been using it at my companies in California.

After a few months of performance reports from marketing came in, Brent went to Gerry and said, "Just get me in front of these people." It was suggested that we pull off a lot of our digital stuff and put it all on direct mail, specifically the tune-up letters that Stochastic sent out.

Gerry looked at the numbers and it looked like it would work, so he did it. We didn't pull completely out of digital, but we pulled out everything that wasn't working. Brent went to town and was running all the tune-ups that were old systems and most likely to be replaced. The sales he generated from that were incredible.

If you don't have a Customer Relationship Management (CRM) system such as ServiceTitan that tracks all your marketing spending and how much revenue you're getting from each campaign, you need to get one. The last time we talked, Tommy Mello from A1 garage door had over 4,000 tracking phone numbers monitoring every campaign he has in his company. My company in California currently has well over 1,000. There is no way to compete today without tracking your marketing expenses. The stakes are just too high.

Gerry came through on driving leads. For branding, he had little plush dogs that looked like our logo to give out on calls. The dogs were adorable and a pleasant surprise. Goettl Air Conditioning Services did something similar way before us. Their brand story features a flashlight, and they weave in a dog named Sadie. If you haven't heard the story, check it out on Goettl Air Conditioning's website. They have mastered story branding. The story goes back to Ken Goodrich working with his dad as a kid, holding the flashlight while his dad worked on Goettl air conditioners. The story is all over the radio, the kid with the flashlight is on the side of their trucks and the story is woven throughout all of their marketing. They give out flashlights and sometimes a plush dog on their service calls. My kids have trick or treated at Ken's house for Halloween and in addition to candy, they each got a flashlight and a plush dog with the Goettl logo on the collar. My kids loved it.

The calls started coming in. The volume wasn't great, but it was enough to get us through the off season and that's all you can ask for. Brent, and Dennis and the team pulled off profits in February and March, beating the budget for net profit by around $35,000 and beating the budget net profit in March by almost $250,000 for the month! I couldn't believe what that team was pulling off.

I went to Fetch-a-Tech every week for nine weeks straight, but by this point, they were running on their own and I was simply providing input. The team was doing things that no one thought were possible. I was blown away.

Chapter Fifteen

ONCE AGAIN, LOOSE LIPS SINK SHIPS - AND DEALS!

The Spring was approaching, and we were all blown away by what had transpired thus far. All we had to do now was not screw up. I couldn't help but smile every time I landed in Vegas. This time, I was flying in because of a tip I got on a Vegas company that might be willing to sell. This would be the cherry on top of the deal; a fourth company that we could acquire. This was a different type of deal. They were profitable. They had long-standing customers with a good track record. The company was called Cal Air. Once again, Gerry had introduced me to a guy named Matt Ballard. Matt used to work for an HVAC supplier and knew everyone, including Cal, who owned the company. Gerry and Matt assured me that this company was a little diamond in the rough that we call Las Vegas.

There was one more piece of this puzzle that made the deal even better. Gerry and Brent both told me that

Ken Goodrich had been wanting to buy it and tuck Cal Air into Goettl for years. I don't know if that was true, but if Ken actually wanted it, then it had to be worth something.

Ken Goodrich is an icon in the Vegas home services market and, quite frankly, an icon in residential home services across the country. He built a company in Las Vegas called Yes Air Conditioning that he would later sell to a large company called ARS. Yes, is still one of the largest companies in Vegas. Then he bought Goettl from ARS, and it has multiple locations, including one in Las Vegas. He grew Goettl to be most likely the largest home services company in Vegas, and he has since sold that as well, but he retains some ownership.

Ken and I met a long time ago when he flew into Fresno, California to look at my company, Lee's Air, to potentially buy it. He flew in on his private jet and I picked him up in my beat-up Ford F-150. I had heard all kinds of stories about him and most were not good, but then most of the stories were told by former disgruntled employees who obviously had some bias.

At lunch that day, I asked Ken about the stories and he talked me through them. We had some good laughs because some were hilarious. If you ever meet Ken, ask him about the pig valve. It's a good one.

The stories I was interested in were how he pulled off these deals. He would find a company that was going to go under because it was in too much debt to their supplier and was, therefore, almost worthless to most people. Then he would convince the supplier to forgive that company's debt if he bought the company. He ended up keeping the company and its owners out of bankruptcy. The supplier got to get a good customer that would buy from them in the future, and Ken got a viable company for almost nothing. It seems obvious in hindsight, but most people don't see those opportunities. They just see a company that's almost bankrupt.

As for Ken's stories, he should be the one to tell them. I will say this: he has a reputation for pushing people's buttons during deals when he was younger. Some of those stories are the most entertaining. I have things I did too when I was young and a lot dumber. I once had a competitor in Fresno and one year I had beaten his revenue numbers. He was constantly teasing about how big his company was. The first year we surpassed his revenue, I bought a book Selling for Dummies. For Christmas, I wrapped it up and took it to his office and gave it to him. I told him it would be a lot more useful to him than to me because it seemed to be written for his type of people.

I got a good laugh, but he didn't find it nearly as funny. For another competitor, he was constantly talking about how much bigger his shop was than mine. When we surpassed his revenue as well around Christmas time, I couldn't go to his shop to deliver it, so I told him via text about the second-place trophy I got him. Again, he didn't find it as funny as I did. My arrogance and stupidity have come down a little, but not much.

Ken has better stories, but his true brilliance showed through in the creative ways he pulled off deals. He would share this valuable information woven through these funny stories. Most people discounted Ken's brilliance because all they heard were the crazy stories. But I wrote EVERYTHING down. It was like taking a Masterclass from one of the best deal makers in our industry. Ken was kind enough to come to my house and record a couple of hours of our conversations about his deals and how he pulled them off. I posted them on Howarddeals.com under the acquisition guide for everyone to listen to.

Years later, when we did the Fetch-a-Tech deal, people would say, "You did a Ken Goodrich deal." It was an honor to hear that. The biggest honor came from Ken himself. He told a large group in his backyard that I had learned from him when I was younger and then came to Vegas and "did the f——ing deal and executed it perfectly." We were on stage together when he told the story. I loved it.

Tommy Mello has a picture in his building in Phoenix of Michael Phelps, the greatest Olympic swimmer of all time. In the picture, Michael is facing forward and looking at the finish line while his competitor in the next lane over is looking at Michael Phelps, trying to see if he was ahead. The caption says "Losers focus on winners. Winners focus on winning." I was always impressed with that caption. As you may recall, I began this book with it! Don't worry too much about what your competitor is doing or do things just because your competitor is. In the case of the Cal Air deal, I wasn't going to buy it just because I heard Ken wanted it. I just used that intel to give me one more piece of information to tell me how this one was probably worth flying out to see it. I needed to focus on winning and making sure the deal was right for us.

So, I flew out to meet Cal at the Air-Conditioning, Heating and Refrigeration (AHR) conference that was held in Vegas in February 2022. He seemed like a good and honest man. His daughter was there with him. She had worked with him for years and you could tell that she cared about her dad. When I dug into the business, it was definitely what Gerry, Brent, and Matt had told me it would be perfect for us to acquire. If you want to grow quickly, acquiring companies is one good way to do it. We had a mission to grow and sell at an unbelievable pace, and this could be a huge help to accomplish our goal. The greatest part was that we were making pretty big profits. We had enough cash to pay Cal. Plus, if we were short of what we needed, we could get a bank loan since we finally had some profits to make a bank feel more comfortable about writing the loan.

I was really excited. After leaving Vegas, I kept in touch with Cal, and we kept in contact and worked through the numbers and the terms of the agreement. If you have ever tried buying a competitor, you probably know that very few of the deals that you start working, actually go through. I couldn't believe that this one was happening. I couldn't have been happier. This was going to boost our growth rate even more. I felt like I was living in a fairytale.

Then the hammer hit. I got a call from Cal. He was irate. He told me that the deal was off. I couldn't put the pieces together. What went wrong? By the end of the call, Cal had given me all the pieces. Someone on our team had called a CSR at another company and leaked information about the deal. I can't tell you how furious I became. In this case, I knew who it was. I won't release their name here. It's irrelevant. Unfortunately, I shared the information about the deal with a couple of key team members who would be affected by the change. They knew we had to keep it totally confidential. But their pride got to them, and they couldn't help but talk to people. Now Cal's employees were hearing rumors, and it was making him look terrible.

This is how things like this can blow deals. It is simply a lack of maturity. In reality, I shouldn't have shared that information with anyone. I felt like I had to at least tell the other shareholders in the company. We couldn't buy a company without all the shareholders knowing and that was the downfall. In any business, you must take ownership. It all comes back to the owner and in the end, it was my fault. All I could do was apologize to Cal, but it didn't matter. The deal was off just because the information was leaked. Besides that, I had built a lot of trust with Cal, and it was all gone in an instant.

All deals and all sales are based on trust, and I couldn't rebuild that trust with Cal.

In your business, it doesn't matter how excited you are about a deal, you must keep it quiet. It is better for everyone in the end if you simply don't tell anyone until you absolutely must.

The deal fell through in late March. February and March still had done well, and we were headed into the second quarter with a good tailwind. We were way ahead of budget. I was frustrated by the setback, and it showed the lack of experience on our team. I hoped that our inexperience wouldn't hit us hard in the busy season. You must have discipline in everything to hit your maximum potential, and this fumble showed a lack of discipline.

Chapter Sixteen

THE WEIGHT OF THE SUMMER

We had told the Flint group that if they loaned us $500,000 when they gave us their company, we would pay them back in the middle of May. Keep in mind, we had a plumbing division, but most of our revenue came from air conditioning. Most AC companies in Vegas lose money through the spring because it's tough selling air conditioners when it's 70 degrees outside with no humidity. We had used the money for rebranding, new uniforms, and a lot of money was spent on big marketing moves. When I borrowed the money, I felt like there was maybe a 20% chance that we would have the money by May to pay them back. But I knew we would make the money by the end of the summer.

The crazy part is that the team pulled it off. We made all the money back, and I was ready to cut the check. It was beyond any projection that I had ever made. I would love to make this a real nail-biter and say it came down to the last minute, but it wasn't close at all. The team crushed it.

I called the Flint group and told them we had made the deadline. What I heard back from them really took me by surprise. It was Collin, the CEO of the group. He told me to hold on to the money. I was flabbergasted. Why would someone not want $500,000? The answer was simple. He told me that given our growth rates, and how well we were doing, he didn't want to trip us up now. He told me that if I had better things to use it for, then use it. Six months before that, he was signing a company over to us that was losing money, and he was questioning whether we would succeed, but he signed reluctantly because they didn't have many other options. Now he was telling us to keep his money and use it to keep growing the company. The greatest thing was that he wasn't going to charge us interest. He just wanted us to keep building the company as fast as possible.

The Flint Group was making money in every other operation. Their group was solid, and they were great operators. Fortunately, they didn't need the money from us. What I learned that day is that many people have money to invest. Many times, they are looking for places to invest it. Unfortunately, there aren't a lot of places to put money to work that will get a decent return. In Colin's case, he found a place to park it that was turning huge returns for him. He was more than happy to tell us to keep the initial loan.

I would learn later that there is no shortage of money out there to be invested. I had such a small mentality previously. I thought that you basically had to beg people to invest in your company. If you are a solid business operator that shows real returns consistently, people will line up to give you the cash you need for growth. They would much rather have it growing with you than sitting in a mutual fund somewhere, or worse, in a no to low-interest-bearing savings account.

So now I had the money I needed to make even more moves. I wished that the Cal Air deal hadn't fallen through because that $500,000 would have been great to use to help pay for their business, but I was now on the hunt for another one.

In the meantime, the summer was upon us. We had gotten through the off-season making money every month and we were excited, but now, another test was upon us. We knew we could sell. Brent and his team sold AC units throughout the spring, which is one of the hardest times of the year to sell air conditioning. Selling in the summer would be way easier. The next test was handling the volume during a Las Vegas summer.

Capacity planning and operations are where a lot of companies fail. If you are in the plumbing or electrical space, the peaks and valleys of the seasons are a lot smaller. In more seasonal businesses, you must build a company that can expand and contract with the seasons and not lose too much money in the off times. The operation of your business and its structure is a lot like the airframe in the plane. If the sales team is bigger and stronger than the operations team can handle, it's like putting a jet engine on a tiny hobby plane. The thing would rip apart mid-air and fall into hundreds of pieces.

The sales team was running on all cylinders. In that 110-to-115-degree Las Vegas summer, they were selling ten to twelve air conditioning systems a day. The install department was run by a guy named Mario, who was often seen with a phone earpiece in each ear. Mario looked like he was taking two calls at once—one phone in each ear. One call on his cell from a salesperson selling a new install and one office phone in the other ear with a customer with questions about the job. The truth is that during that summer, if we had made any more sales, or put more gas into that engine, the plane would have started to fall apart. The plane was flying as fast as it could, and Mario was single-handedly holding the install department together.

The problem any business owner runs into in this situation is that you have a choice: hire more people to help during this time period and strengthen your operation, allowing you to handle more speed, or let things run as they are and risk catastrophic failure. That usually comes in the form of top salespeople quitting because they can't sell enough jobs because the company is booked solid for installs with no room for more, or customers getting angry because they are waiting too long for their system to be installed.

There is a downside to hiring more people. Your busy season will inevitably come to an end. Then you have the choice of laying off quickly those temporary hires, which usually hurts culture, or trying to hold on to them and possibly killing your profitability in the off season.

Balancing growth and profitability has always been a pain in seasonal businesses. If you manage it well, the profits can be fantastic, but most people don't. One of the key things that I tell people in these situations is that you shouldn't make decisions based on what is happening right in front of you today. Every time I see images of World War II or movies with reenactments of the boats storming the beaches of Normandy, I realize those men were in a terrible situation, with bombs going off all around them and bullets flying at them. I have never been in a situation like that, but I can only imagine that my first reaction, without any training, would be to freeze up. Then, if I had any wits about me and hadn't completely lost my mind, I would probably try to take cover and not get shot.

That's not what they did to take the beach, though. If they all tried to take cover, care for the wounded, or run away from the bullets and bombs, they all would have almost certainly failed. Instead, they had to keep moving forward and get up the beach. They had to look at the big picture. It's staggering to me they pulled it off. While bombs were going off all around them, they moved forward.

In my experience, it's like that in business. You need to have your plan, the budget. You need to keep an eye on how you are going to get there. You can't always react with snap decisions about hiring and firing or responding to a bad customer review with the thing that seems like the immediate solution.

You have to ask yourself questions like these, geared to your particular trade business: Does hiring an install manager to help during busy periods fit into your long-term plan for the year, or does it solve a short-term need but cause long-term problems? I don't know the answer for you in your particular case, but it's a question that needs to be asked and answered. Does that customer complaint need to be solved by you right now, does your current growth necessitate building a process for someone else to handle it, or maybe there was a failure in the process that caused the complaint in the first place that should be remedied? Additional questions you may have to ask and answer.

Many times, as business owners, we react to what is right in front of us, and the problem we see right now, when we really should move up the beach to solve the long-term problem, which is taking out that machine gun nest causing us all these problems in the first place.

One thing you can do, and I highly recommend it, is turning toward automation for help. People complain about software, including ServiceTitan, all the time saying it doesn't do X, Y, or Z, which is part of our workflow. In many cases, your workflow may be better than what is possible in whatever software you are running. Sometimes, and many that I have seen, it simply isn't better and should be done away with, but since the company has been doing it for so long a certain way, they just don't want to change. Then they make a giant manual process outside of their software to accommodate a workflow that is flawed in the first place. Or maybe the workflow is better, but they don't see the real expense that the manual effort is costing the company.

I have observed that when you have an automated workflow, that part of it doesn't care how big you get in the busy season or how small you get in the off season. It just runs. It drastically reduces management's workload and stress when they are trying to hire and lay off in different seasons. It also takes away the problem of reducing profitability in the off season because you can't keep people on the payroll that you never hired in the first place.

One simple process that requires someone to export an Excel sheet and copy and paste it into a spreadsheet once a day is WAY more costly than you think. In the heat of the busy season, that person has a hundred things to do, and that copy and pasting required activity will sometimes be missed. Then, if that copy and paste person quits or is terminated, you must hire someone else and train him or her on how to do it, and then he or she will pick up all the other things that must be learned and the cycle will continue. Instead, I suggest you automate, automate, automate.

With our one man Install management team, it made sense to keep him operating continually as if it was during the summertime. We couldn't automate him away, but we tried to automate everything around him. Dennis, the GM, was checking on him daily, but he was making it through the slower times.

Chapter Seventeen

HIRING FAMILY

I really hate hiring family members and I avoid it as much as possible. There are too many problems that may arise from it. Most business owners think it is because they worry about the weird conversations that will have to happen around the table at Thanksgiving dinner after a bad performance review, or maybe a lot of family drama might unfold if you have to fire them.

The consequences of hiring family members are much worse than that. Most of the time, business owners either don't have the guts to write that bad performance review of their family member, or they don't fire that underperforming sibling. Then that family member is there to sit like a cancer, slowly rotting away the business from the inside out. At the very least, they simply underperform and are taking the spot of someone who could perform and drive the business forward. At the worst, they are belligerent and getting too comfortable knowing that they won't get fired, sowing seeds of contempt among your staff. It is likely that the rest of the staff will lose respect for the owner because they know that he or she simply isn't strong enough of a leader to make the right call and fire their family member. If you are a business owner, ask yourself these questions: How many times have you put off giving a bad performance review to a regular employee that you are not related to? How many times have you at least written the review in a way that wasn't as direct and to the point as it should have been because you didn't want to have that fight? If you are honest with yourself, it has happened a lot. It happens to all of us. Now, think about how much harder it would be when you have a family or close friend relationship with that person outside of work. You may not even be conscious of what you are doing. It may be worse. You may believe you're not treating them differently from the other employees when, in fact, you are and the entire team knows you are.

Any business owner or manager that has had employees longer than fifteen minutes has probably looked the other way when poor performance has happened in their company. Maybe the top salesperson who has been blowing off company meetings or maybe treating another employee with disrespect, but you were afraid of losing sales if he quit, so you said nothing to him or her. Maybe the top customer service rep with the highest call booking rate that shows up fifteen minutes late regularly, but you don't want to rock the boat too much in your CSR department, so you say nothing. If this is the case for you, and be totally honest with yourself if it is, then fix it now. That top salesperson or top CSR can be replaced. If you aren't willing to do it, you cannot grow your business on a larger scale, and you simply are not a good operator and your employees deserve better.

Fix it and get better or get out of the way and put someone else in charge who is willing to be the leader you should have been. Your employees will be grateful and perform a lot better when they see you step up and make the change. I assure you. If you aren't writing performance reviews, then start now! It costs you almost nothing and will be a great step in the right direction for your business.

When Hiring a Family Member Pays Off

In the previous November, right before we acquired CCE, I needed someone to go to Armenia to build out the call center for my other company, Lee's Air. Starting a remote call center is easy. Making one that is truly effective is hard. Most people can't get it right, and they give up and drop it. My sister, Kathryn, is a five-time convicted felon. She has trafficked drugs on a large scale, and I did no business of any kind with her for years. She had been out of prison for 10 years and was looking for a job or another project. She was incredible at sales, obviously, and a great call center is basically a sales organization in its own right. I got a crazy idea and asked her to go to Armenia and live there for six months, training and working in my call center. It had only two employees, and I wanted it to grow to about ten. They would pick up the phones at 8 p.m. California time and go until noon the next day. Our California team would come online at 7 a.m. That gave me double coverage from 7 a.m. to noon and my staff in California would come back from lunch when Armenia was going offline.

Kathryn went to California and trained for two weeks on the trades and how our call center was supposed to work in California. Then she hopped on the next flight to Armenia.

She did far better than I had hoped. She had multiple CSRs getting higher call booking rates than some of the CSRs in the US. She went to restaurants and hired waiters. She went on museum tours and hired the tour guide. She found all kinds of people who spoke English well and had customer service skills and brought them in. I listened to one call. The customer said, "I notice an accent. Are you in some remote call center overseas?" The agent, following the script that Kathryn wrote, immediately responded with, "Ma'am, I speak five languages. Here at Lee's, they look for multi-lingual people. That way, we can serve all the Fresno area."

The customer responded with nothing but praise saying how appreciative she was that Lee's would do something like that. The funniest part was that CSR did speak five languages, but 52% of Fresno is Hispanic and we still don't have anyone in Armenia that speaks Spanish. I had to laugh, but the script worked well and in 2023, six of the eleven CSRs that received awards at the Lee's awards banquet for the top call booking rates were based in Armenia.

When my sister Kathryn was finished in Armenia and the operation was running smoothly, she headed back to the U.S. and asked if I had anything else. At first, I said no. I had paid her for the project and wasn't looking to put her on a team just to give her a job. Then a couple of weeks later, Dennis called and was having issues in the call center. I thought about it for a few minutes and referred him to Kathryn. He was skeptical because of her history. I told him he could call her and if it didn't work out, it was fine by me, and he could fire her at any time. That gave him peace of mind, and he hired her.

If you have a GM or a manager, please empower them to make their own decisions. They will own their decision and own the results of their decisions. They will appreciate you for it, even if the outcome is poor and they must fix it. You will also appreciate the results. Just hold them to the performance standards that you need to and let them operate inside those parameters.

Kathryn is the only family member that I have employed besides my wife and brother. I only had my wife working for me for a few months while we were in a rough spot and needed someone to fill in for a short time. We had multiple arguments when she would show up late and I couldn't let the team see that showing up late was ok. My brother worked for me as an install helper for a few months in the summer for one year. There are occasions where your family member or long-time friend are great fits for a position, but if you want hiring a family member to work for you and your company, do everything you can to hold them to the same standards that you do for everyone else. Kathryn started working at Fetch-a-Tech in June. She really helped turn things around in the call center in Las Vegas. Dennis appeared to be happy with her performance. Then, after a few months of working there and the heat of the summer was winding down in late September, the Service Manager was having some issues. He asked Kathryn to run the morning training meeting with the service technicians. It was the night before the meeting, and she had never been a service technician before or done any technical work, for that matter. She saw that as a minor detail. She showed up for the training the next morning and decided to do the training on the thing she knew best, sales.

Dennis attended the training. I don't know if he was going there to learn something, if he thought this was going to be amusing, or he was just curious about what in the world she was going to talk about. A few minutes into the training, a technician walked in late. She asked him why he came in late and he said that he was the highest selling technician in the whole company and had sold 300,000 dollars in the month of August so he didn't need the sales training. She said "Oh, 300,000 dollars, that's cute. You sold 300,000 dollars' worth of Air Conditioning in August to people in Las Vegas in

110-degree weather. I sold more than 300,000 dollars' worth of weight loss products online last month and I am a fat chick. So how about you sit down, shut up, and quit being disruptive and learn a thing or two." Once the laughter calmed down, she had everyone's attention, and Dennis was astonished. A day or two later, he promoted her to become the service manager. She ended up enrolling in HVAC tech school right afterward and the following month, October, the average ticket in the service department doubled. In fact, the top tech ended up selling 800,000 dollars that October, in moderate weather after selling 300,000 dollars in August when it was 110 degrees outside.

Dennis was taking a pretty big risk by putting someone in the service manager position who had never run a single service call before, but he saw what was really important there, which was leadership, customer service, and sales ability. The technical stuff can be taught much easier than the rest of those things. He took a risk, and it paid off.

Chapter Eighteen

RUNNING THE PROCESS

NOTE: If you don't own a business and never will,
or you never want to sell your business,
you may want to skip this chapter.

As we got into the summer and were coming out of it and heading to the Fall, we were neck deep in preparing the company for sale. We were constantly keeping our eye on the goal of getting the company very profitable in that first year and having it packaged for sale.

When you go to sell your trades business with over $1 million in annual net profit, I highly recommend using a broker and going through a traditional process. It is called Running the Process for a reason. You don't wake up one day and decide to sell your business and then sell the company the next day. The process takes time and if you run the whole process and don't cut corners, you generally get the best price and partner for your business that you can.

Typically, you talk to a broker who has sold businesses in your industry before. We selected Wayne

Twardokus from League Park. There are several out there, but Wayne was the one we found to be best for our needs at the time. Others include Fred from SF&P advisors and Eric Van Dam from Piper Sandler. They each target different companies of different sizes and provide different services. There are more, but I know these people personally and have worked with all three of them. I'm comfortable putting their names in this book. I receive no compensation for doing so, but I wanted to help people who don't even know where to start when selling your business.

When you retain or hire a broker, there are two things you can do. You can have them look at your financials and do some light verification and then take the company to market and they will handle marketing it for you. If you go this route, they will make slide decks and presentations and make the company look as impressive as possible. They will market it to potential buyers and then you will, hopefully, receive multiple offers. Those offers are called letters or intent. It's a letter that says that based on your financials we intend to buy your company for xx amount of money, let's say it's $10 million dollars, and we expect to close on x date, let's say January 30th or whatever dollar amount and date they come up with. You will then have to choose which buyer to go with.

I will talk about choosing a buyer later in more detail, but for now, keep in mind that you are really choosing a partner. Then you sign the letter of intent from the buyer that you chose. The buyer will start what is called due diligence. Due diligence is when they go over your financials with a fine-tooth comb. It usually takes about three months. If you haven't been through this before, it is a lot like getting a colonoscopy every day for 90 days, but you are wide awake and completely aware of everything they're looking for. During this time, investigators will discover anything you may have intentionally or unintentionally hidden in your business.

If they find anything significant, they will come back to you and at least expect concessions on the deal and offer a price lower than what the letter of intent stated, or they will walk away from the deal altogether.

There is another thing you can do though that I highly recommend. Have your financials audited ahead of time, before you even meet with a broker or in the beginning talks with them, by a third-party accounting firm. We call this "Quality of Earnings." If your sale is large enough, have it done by one of the big four accounting firms. This can be costly. At Fetch, we chose a smaller company called Guardian Due Diligence out of Michigan. Elliott is the owner and has helped me a lot. It may cost you between $30,000 and $100,000 to have a smaller company do it, but in the long run, it will be worth every penny. They will find your dirty secrets well ahead of time and you get to correct them and clean them up before you even show your financials to any prospective buyers. If you do this, when you accept an offer and go into diligence, you can rest reasonably assured that you aren't going to look stupid during diligence and that you will get the full amount that was written on the letter of intent.

At Fetch, we went this route. You should expect that the Quality of Earnings (Q of E) period will take a few months, so we started this while the summer was coming to an end. We still had several months of performance that we had to prove ourselves on, but we had to get this out of the way. After the Q of E was complete, each month that we closed after that, they could quickly go back and verify the earnings of that one month in a couple of days, so we would be up to date.

If you are planning on selling your business, having a rough idea of the process and how long everything takes is critical to being able to get it done and to hitting your target deadline. We still had a long way to go, but we were more than halfway there, and by the end of the summer, I projected we would hit $4.5 million profit for the year. The team was way out-performing their goals, and I couldn't have been happier.

Chapter Nineteen

TIME IS TICKING

In the summer, I started to notice trends across the country. The price of companies had skyrocketed. It looked like 2006 when housing pricing was skyrocketing right before the fall of the housing crisis. If you had a house during that time, it was like sitting at the top of a rollercoaster and you were about to have the drop of a lifetime. But I was worried about Fetch. We needed to show twelve months of strong earnings before we could sell it, but the pressure in the market was mounting. Owners and operators were being bought out of their companies and leaving, and I was worried about the ability of these companies to run after they left.

I was so worried about it I flew down to Phoenix to meet Tommy Mello, owner of A1 Garage Door. I had previously told him to never sell, but this time, my tone was different. I told him he had to sell. We were at a restaurant, and he thought I was crazy.

I went back to his house, and I turned on a movie called *The Big Short*. It was all about the financial crisis of 2008.

The next morning, he called his team and started prepping the company for sale. It would end up being a monster deal with the buyer being Cortec, that had previously bought the brand Yeti. It would be a great deal for both parties, but the sale prices of businesses his size dropped a few months after he sold. I was really happy it didn't go the other way. I would have felt bad.

The year 2006 was insane. We had banks giving home loans to people with no income, no job, and no assets to use as collateral. Those mortgages were all packaged and sold as bonds with the ratings agencies giving them great ratings as prime bonds.

There is a lot to the 2008 financial crisis, and it gets very complicated. I studied it a lot. I will leave it at this. In late 2022, we didn't have the massive issues that we had in 2006. I was really concerned about the multiples on profit that private equity companies were willing to pay moving forward. I was worried prices were going to come down dramatically.

The problem was that we weren't ready to sell even though the pressure was on to move as fast as possible. We had to get Fetch-a-Tech across the line and put the money in our pockets.

Chapter Twenty

A SURPRISE PHONE CALL

I was at my house in Southern California when I got a call that I wasn't expecting. It was Cal from Cal Air. Cal Air was the company I tried to buy earlier in the year, but the deal fell through because someone on my team had talked about it and let the word out. I was fully expecting him to tell me he had heard something else that we had leaked, but he didn't. Instead, he was cordial and happy. We exchanged pleasantries, and I wanted to know what he was getting at. He was giving me another shot at his company, but there was one caveat. He wanted me to keep it completely quiet and keep the deal just between him and me.

I didn't know what to say. The problem I had was that I only owned 26.6% of the company, but he wanted me to decide about acquiring a company that would cost us millions of dollars without telling anyone. Working at ServiceTitan, I have been known to be a bit of a maverick, and if I know something is a good idea, I will push my way around until I can get it done. In this case, even if I could wrap my head around the ethics of it all, I would still have to get the company integrated into Fetch. This usually takes at least a month and that is assuming the team has time and knows it's coming and can prepare.

Then, if I could pull the deal off, how would my team react, knowing that I withheld information from them for months? They would be furious! Then there is the timeline issue. Cal called me in August to start discussions up again about the deal. We were planning on selling the company at the end of the year. I knew we needed to have everything completely integrated, and we needed time to put some profit to the bottom line as well. We knew we could add profit, but every day counted at this point.

For those of you tucking companies into your business, as long as the company is fully integrated into your company during the sale process, they will usually give you credit for the profit that the company you acquired earned for that year. Cal Air was a solid company, with profit that we could count towards our EBITDA, but we wanted to be able to capitalize on it. We did not just want credit for what they had already done. We wanted to get in there, find some efficiencies and outbound call their database and start driving sales higher than they would have if we hadn't bought it. We had a large call center by that point, and I knew we could do it, but there was very little time!

I told Cal that I had to think about his offer, and I got off the phone.

That afternoon, I realized that one move would solve most of my problems. I called Cal back and said, "Ok, we can do the deal, but we need this done in a couple weeks. I will trust your financials and move at lightning speed."

He was good with it. It would speed up the process and I wouldn't have to feel like I was lying or hiding anything from my team for too long, so they would be less mad when they heard about the deal. Then, it would give me more time to get the database integrated and Cal Air's phone numbers forwarded to our ServiceTitan account. That would give our team, including Brent Buckley and our call center, a lot more time to work with our database on sales and outbound calling and help our profits.

The risk to all this was that if Cal was deceitful in any way, or if his accountant wasn't very good, and the financials weren't what he said that they were, I would be in big trouble. I trusted Cal implicitly, and this was the only way I could see getting the deal done. So, I went for it.

I called Elliott from Guardian, who was on my Quality of Earnings, and asked him to do an overview of the financials, just to get a quick check. He verified what he could about Cal Air in that short time frame, and we moved forward.

A week before the deal for Cal Air was ready, I had to call Gerry. I got permission from Cal to do it. Gerry still had control over all the marketing. I was ready for him to be frustrated, but he was ecstatic. Giving him a database that had been well taken care of for years was like handing ten pounds of chocolate to a seven-year-old kid.

Gerry got to work with their database and moved fast. This was also strategic for me because Gerry held 26.6% of the shares as well. This meant that if he approved, which he did, I had the votes between the two of us to get the sale approved.

The next calls were going to be the hard ones. I had to tell Brent and Dennis. I was feeling guilty because I felt like I should have told them sooner. It was weighing heavily on me. I couldn't wait to tell them because I just wanted the weight off my shoulders. Cal agreed I could tell them 24 hours before the deal closed.

Brent, Dennis, and I went to lunch, and I gave them the news. Dennis took it well. Brent liked the idea, but I could tell that he had reservations. He looked at me as if I had just done something sneaky and had gotten caught. What I had done was sneaky, and I wasn't proud of it. But in the end, it was the best thing for the team, and everyone understood that.

The greatest news was that we had made a lot of profit by that point and had millions in cash in the bank. I was able to do the Cal Air deal in cash only, with no shares being issued to Cal, which meant that no one was getting diluted by this deal.

A lot of business owners like to take dividends or draws throughout the year. I have never been a fan of that. There are reasons to take money out of your corporation to protect the funds, but in most cases, owners take out more than they should, or they just have bad spending habits. If we had done that, the Cal Air deal wouldn't have happened, because we wouldn't have had the cash necessary to do the deal.

There is something about the Cal Air deal and how we structured it that may interest you. Whenever you are doing a small deal like this, one thing you can do is split the payments on the business. The best-case scenario for you is that you don't pay any money up front and then you sign a contract that is essentially a note payable to the seller and you can pay them monthly for their business over time. Cal wasn't interested in that, but he was concerned about taxes. I offered to pay him half up front in September and half on January 1st. That way, he could split the payments over two tax years and reduce his tax liability. It also gave me an interest free loan for about four months. It worked out for both of us. I really love deals like that where everyone benefits.

After lunch that day, Cal and his wife were smiling, and they both shook my hand. I was elated that we had done this deal together and that they knew they trusted me. After our history, that meant a lot to me. We left the lunch meeting and went on our way. The next day, the deal closed and Cal announced it to his team. It was all hands-on deck at the Fetch office, trying to integrate at lightning speed. I was thrilled to hand Gerry, Brent and Dennis a new database and company to work with. They hopped on it and made the best of it in no time. Having a team like that is a dream.

Chapter Twenty-One

IDEAS FOR YOUR OWN TUCK-INS

I'm often asked that when it comes to tuck-ins, how do we do it without losing their customers? (As you probably know, a "tuck'in" is the term for when another company, which is usually a larger one, acquires another company, generally a smaller one, and absorbs it into their company.) I also get asked about how you make money on those customers, because usually the previous company didn't charge enough and they were having financial troubles, which is why they needed to be bought out.

Whenever we tuck-in a business, we do a few things:

1. The first thing we do is forward the business' phone number to your office. I highly recommend doing this through ServiceTitan, so you can track all the revenue that comes from the people that call in from that number. This makes it super easy to see the return on

your investment on that tuck-in. After you do one or two of these, and you see the returns, it will make you a lot more confident to do more in the future.

2. When a customer from the previous company calls your office, the customer usually says, "I was looking for XYZ Air, what happened to them?" The first thing you need to say to them is, "You called the right place." Do that right away to buy yourself time to explain the situation before they hang up on you. Then you have a set script for the CSR. The CSR would usually say something to the effect of "Mr. and Ms. Jones were the owners of that company, and they retired and entrusted us to honor their warranties and take care of their customers and their employees. Their employees work here now. I can get you set up. What's going on at your home?" You can even offer to send their favorite tech if they had one and he or she still works for you.

3. Pull a list of all the customers in their database and do a mass mailing. Include a letter explaining that you merged the companies together after Mr. and Mrs. Jones retired. Tell them that Mr. and Mrs. Jones entrusted you to take care of their customers and to do that, you would like to send them

coupons with discounts. Include coupons for a discounted tune-up, money off a water heater flush, a free plumbing inspection, and whatever else would be relevant to almost any homeowner even if nothing in their house is broken. For example, even though I am an HVAC tech, I will not service my own AC unit. I always pay someone else to do it whenever I remember it. I would love to have someone come check all the valves under all my sinks. That way, I don't have to crawl under there myself and remember to do it before I get another nasty drip under my vanity that causes mold and other things. In California, I bought a company called Vern's plumbing. We spent $1,600 dollars sending a letter to all their relatively recent customers with this exact approach. With that one letter, we generated $170,000 dollars in revenue! Always use a tracking phone number in ServiceTitan for these so you can track the return on your efforts.

4. Charge your normal prices. We retain about 85% of the customers on average from our tuck-ins. We just charge our normal prices. Most of their customers would have probably paid the higher prices anyway and the old company was just too afraid to ask for the

money. Charge what you need to charge. The exception to this is new construction and some commercial accounts. You need to charge what is necessary, but since they do a ton of volume and just want the basics all the time, they may stop being your customer. You need to be ok with that. I did a tuck-in one time that was 30% commercial, and I shut down the commercial department the next day. It wasn't worth my time. Sometimes, it is, but you need to make that call.

5. Get your call center doing outbound calling to the database. Call them up and have a basic script ready. Tell them that the company was recently merged and that they get one free tune-up or inspection or something after the merger. Do not wait for your letter to work or for them to have a problem. Be proactive and make it happen.

6. In most cases, if the company had a minor brand, re-wrap their trucks right away. Don't wait. If they had a large presence in your area, re-wrap them, but put a magnet on the side so that the wrap is your standard wrap and then the magnet reads: "Partnered with XYZ Company." That way, after about a year, you can remove the magnet, and you will be completely migrated over.

People complain all the time that their tuck-ins didn't work out, and that they didn't make any money. In my experience, I have never lost money on a tuck-in. They are some of my favorite acquisitions. You have to do two things, though. You need to get them for a decent price, and you need to work the database immediately, and be proactive about it. If you need help on figuring out how to price a tuck-in, there are resources on our website **howarddeals.com** to help with that.

Chapter Twenty-Two

IT'S A MARATHON, NOT A SPRINT

After the summer wrapped up, we were working on the Cal Air merger and heading into October. You could tell that things had settled down. The summer's full-steam pace was over, and now the company's employees were significantly calmer. In these cases, I tell all of my staff to remember that you are running a marathon, not a sprint. It is very easy to think "Hey, we're ahead of budget, we can slow down." But those words will kill your business. If you do that, it's a recipe for disaster.

For instance, in the call center, when the inbound call volume slows down, the call center can't let up. The goal should not be to answer every call that comes in. The goal of the call center should be to make sure a certain number of calls are on the board every day. If that is the goal, then when the inbound calls slow down, the outbound calls must increase to make up the difference.

By the end of the September, we were pretty sure that we were going to hit $5 million in EBITDA for the year.

We were also confident that we could get at least ten times profit for the sale of the business, which was way more than I had told people we would get. We were all pretty happy. The team didn't let up, though, and they kept running.

We had the Cal Air database, and we had to move. If we had let up then, we would have left a lot of money on the table. Once I had closed the Cal Air deal, I wasn't in the office much after that. Dennis, Brent, Gerry, and team took the new acquisition, including the database, and dug in. I stood on the sidelines and got out of the way.

When you reach this point in your progress with a sale, it's very easy for owners to stop caring about what happens in their business. People ask me how they should operate it if they are selling and if they should do anything differently. With a few exceptions, run it as if you were going to own it for another ten years. No one wants to buy a business where the owner checked out months before the close. They also don't want to buy a business where you laid off key people to make your numbers look good just before the sale.

I wouldn't be able to sleep at night knowing that I did that to someone I was selling to. Second, it's a small industry and word will get out about what kind of deals I have done in the past. I wouldn't want my name coming up in a conversation like that. I need to look people in the eye after a deal and I want them to know that if they do a deal with me in the future, that they will get a good company from me. So run through the finish line, don't let up. It's easy to get tempted to let up, but it's not worth it.

Chapter Twenty-Three

FETCHING THE OFFERS

As we turned the corner and left the Fall, heading into the winter, we had a wind in our sails. We couldn't believe it. We had beaten all our expectations. We were headed straight towards $6 million in adjusted profit/ EBITDA. I was looking at the numbers almost daily and there was no one more surprised than me. I couldn't believe it. The quality of earnings was done, and the numbers were clean. When you are doing a deal like this, the Quality of Earnings reports get done, but then each month that you close after that, have to be analyzed as well. After our month end closed, I would hear from the third-party firm that we were on track and the numbers were validated. I was certain that the numbers we were giving the broker were accurate. I wouldn't have believed it was true if it had not been for that firm doing the audit every month now. The team was performing beyond our beliefs.

While your Quality of Earnings is being done, your broker is usually setting up what we call the data room and the deck. They put together a nice presentation that shows off the key pieces of your company and the data is there to show a potential buyer whatever they would need to make you an offer.

Putting all this paperwork together is a pain, but it is well worth it. Having a good broker is key in this situation. They know what to gather, what buyers are interested in, and how to present it. Almost all the data that they need can come from your accountant and your general manager. It's important to know that during this time, it will add additional load onto your accountant and senior leadership. I believe that setting expectations with them ahead of time goes a long way. No one wants to come to work thinking that things will be smooth that day and then find out that it is much harder than expected. If you make it sound terrible and then it's not as bad as they originally thought, you get the same amount of work done, but with a lot less anger and frustration on their part.

As soon as it's all collected, the broker goes to work presenting your company to potential buyers. We had a lot of interest early on, but there were a few things that the buyers didn't like. This may bore for you, but if you are ever planning on selling your business, it's good to know about them so you can think about them and potentially fix them before you go to market.

First, they didn't like that we only had one year of earnings to show. There was not much that I could have done to change this except hold on for another year or longer. The flux capacitor was broken on my time machine.

There wasn't much else I could do with that and still make it to market on time and get cash in our pockets on time.

Second, they all noticed that 50% of our revenue was sold by Brent Buckley. This was a big problem for many of them. You do not want your company relying on any single employee like that. The hard part about that was that Brent was really good at what he did, and I surely was not going to tell him to sell less. The best thing you can do is try to train others in your company to sell more. If we had done that more effectively, we wouldn't have had that objection hit us nearly as hard as it did. Two buyers wouldn't even give us an offer because of it. I just assumed that they would give us a lower offer but instead, but they just didn't give us one at all.

Other things to look out for that we didn't have an issue with, but are worth mentioning are:

- Try not to have a lot of your revenue tied up with one customer. This happens a lot in the commercial and construction space. You may have one client that represents 30% of your revenue. A private equity firm looking to buy your company would look at that and see it as quite a big risk. They know that if that one customer leaves, that you are going to take a big hit.

- Don't have a management team that is so thin that you can't grow. If you ran your staff into the ground thinking you wouldn't have to hire anyone and you could keep your costs down, they will simply add on extra costs in their forecasts because they will plan on hiring more people to run your operation sustainably. In this case, you may as well have just hired them ahead of time. Don't drive your staff crazy before the sale, since they aren't going to give you credit for that savings, anyway.

The good news was that there were plenty of other companies that were willing to participate in our process, even with the risks they saw.

The broker will find out who is really interested and serious about making an offer and then they will schedule management meetings. This is when the potential buyers will come in and meet with your top managers and potentially with you as well. A good broker will sit with you ahead of time and coach you on what to say in these meetings and what not to say. The main thing that they will tell you is to answer the questions that they are asking and in as concise a way as possible. Avoid pontificating on things and going off on tangents and talking about how great you are, etc. If your company is performing, then they will know that you are great. Let the numbers speak for themselves. They do a lot of these management meetings and it's a waste of your time and theirs to go off on tangents.

Be friendly. This is not a time to sit with your arms crossed and say things such as, "You'd better give me a good offer, or we aren't going with you." It's a sales process and they know that you have a broker or banker representing you and if your company and broker are even halfway decent, then you will be getting multiple offers. They will have to give you a good offer for you to accept it. There is no reason to be a jackass here.

This is a two-way interview. You are interviewing them, and they are interviewing you. You are looking for a solid partner or buyer, and they are looking for an upstanding business person they can trust. Leave the hardline and extravagant negotiation tactics for the movies because that is the only place where they work. I did not even go to the management meetings. That was tactical on my part. I had spent no time running the company. I wanted the team to prove that to the potential buyers. If the buyer believes that someone is key to the operation, then they will want to build the deal so that the key individuals must stay. They usually do this by setting up golden handcuffs for key people. These golden handcuffs come in the form of earnouts where, if you perform well, you get paid more over time. For instance, you get paid a certain amount for your company up front, but then if the company performs well in the first year after the acquisition, then you get another payday. Usually, they discount the first payment for your business and put the rest of it on the earn out.

There are also things that keep you around, such as an equity payout. They may offer you stock in their company if you stay. This means that if you perform well, you get a stock payout and when their company sells, you get another payout. There are a lot of ways that they do it, but they are many types of golden handcuffs. They aren't all that bad. They are called golden for a reason. I just wasn't looking to be tied up at all.

After the management meetings, each firm goes back and puts their offer together and they send it over to your broker. In this stage, as I've mentioned before, the offers come in the form of a Letter of Intent (LOI). You may get one or two or ten of these. Then again, you may get none. The letter includes everything that they want to offer you for your business. It will place a value on your business. You will sort through them and figure out which one that you want to take. In my case, with a few partners involved, this was a little more complicated than it is for someone who is the only owner of the business.

We received four offers. I can't tell you how exciting it was to have spent over a year working towards this moment and then realizing that our plan was coming to fruition. We had real offers on the table. Our final EBITDA was a little over $6 million! I can't say what the offers were, but at the time of writing this book, there was a website showing average multiples of profit paid for privately held HVAC companies. The website is https://firstpagesage.com/business/hvac-ebitda-valuation-multiples. It shows in 2025, the multiples were around 10.8 times profit for residential company doing heating and cooling work. That would have put our valuation at $6 million in EBITDA times 10.8 which would put it at $64.8 million. Due to a non-disclosure agreement, I cannot reveal the actual number, but that is what the going rate was. I couldn't believe my eyes. In basically one year, we built well over $50 million in value. We had the plan, but the team blew the plan out of the water and even when we got toward the end, I still couldn't believe it.

Now was the hard part. We had to pick one. You would think this would have been easy, but it wasn't. We had agreed that we wouldn't just take the highest offer. We said that we would take the top three and then the people who were going to have to stay and work on the business and truly be partners with the people buying the business, should be able to decide about which company to work with.

A company that was trying to get into the home service space made the highest offer. They knew nothing about how to run a home service business and when the management team at Fetch asked them about their plan, they said that they hoped that we would have the plan. They put in the highest cash offer, but the management team did not want to move forward with them.

In this case, their offer would have gotten me an extra couple million dollars in the short term. In the long run, it probably would have given me less. The point is that the team made a wise decision. I was really proud of being part of a team that was willing to make a tough call like that when there was a lot of money on the line. They acted in their long-term best interests and the best interests of their employees. That's hard to do when there is that kind of money on the line.

They chose the second highest offer. It was from Service Champions from Southern California. They had a long track record of buying companies like ours. They also had a track record of maintaining and growing profits. They were a great company, and we really lucked out. They worked with us through the entire sales process and were very reasonable. When you are choosing a company to work with, it's a lot like getting married. Once you make your decision, you make a commitment to make the relationship work. In business, you don't get to go back and get a redo. Choose wisely!

Chapter Twenty-Four

DUE DILIGENCE: THE DAILY COLONOSCOPY

It feels like such a relief when those letters of intent come in and you pick one and sign it. For a brief period, it seems like the courtship is over and that the marriage has begun. But instead of going on a honeymoon, you get to go through the arduous process of what's known as due diligence. I call it the daily colonoscopy because you feel like you are getting inspected, unwillingly, daily for about three months. The biggest load will be on your accountants, and the second biggest load will be on your management team.

If you're wondering what I'm talking about, let me explain. The buyers start asking for things that you probably have never thought of, or ever used, such as copies of your articles of incorporation. If you have ever had a lawsuit, they will want to know all the details. The best thing to do here is to have a great legal team that will be johnny-on- the-spot when those requests come through.

Our due diligence process got complicated a couple of times. The more partners you have, the more eventful this entire process may become. We had a law firm representing us. They had around ten attorneys working on our side at any given moment. This is critical because when you are doing a deal of this size. The other side may send over a 100-page document and in order to stay on track, you have to read it, redline it, and send it back in a day or so. They must split work among many attorneys if they are going to get something like that done in a timely manner. It was not uncommon to get emails from our attorneys at two in the morning, especially as we got close to closing day. The craziest part was that the opposing counsel would respond to them in minutes. I couldn't believe the hours that these people worked to get our deal done.

I found out that the partners didn't feel they were being represented well. I could see their point. They didn't know the attorneys, and they felt like they needed their own representation. I told them they couldn't just change attorneys on a whim. The attorneys we were using had done similar deals multiple times before, and they were quite good. I But that wasn't changing their opinion. I was freaking out. They didn't understand the magnitude of what was happening. They wanted their own local Vegas attorney to represent their interests.

As a last, desperate plea, the broker and Collin came up with an idea. Their attorney could represent them on their employment agreements with the new company, but we would keep the attorneys we were using for the sale of the stock. They agreed, and we moved forward. My heart rate calmed way down after that. I look back now at what we were doing and I realize that if Collin and Wayne, the Broker, hadn't come up with that idea, we would have had to change legal counsel. Their attorney owned a small law office in Vegas. The process would have taken a year to get across the finish line. I am getting PTSD just writing about this.

If your partners have been through a sale process before, they will be a lot more understanding, but this was a first for most of the partners. I should have tried to explain things better to them, but it seemed like every time I turned around, they felt I was screwing them. I wanted it all to be over, but there was such a long way to go. I was getting physically ill from all the stress.

But this process is necessary if you want to command the real money. Stay strong, hang in there, and you will get through it.

Chapter Twenty-Five

THE LAUNCH

At the end of diligence, it is time to close and finalize the transaction. The process ran me into the ground. The last few days of the deal are stressful, to say the least. This deal was, by far, the most stressful one I have ever been through. When you have a lot of partners, it always is, but when you have a lot of partners who have never been through it before and it represents a large amount of their net worth, it's like a roller coaster of stress.

There were at least three times that someone threatened to pull the plug on the whole deal. In one case, it was about one employee's earnout versus another. One person was getting advice from another plumber who had sold his business and took that advice as gospel. I had represented several companies in sales before and some of the advice this plumber was giving was simply false, but there was no convincing our employee that the advice was terrible.

He would say, "What are you worried about, Tom? We can just go back on the market."

That's partially true, but once you break an LOI, you get a black mark and that means a lot of private equity groups will no longer take you seriously. Not to mention that you have to start the entire sales process all over again and go through the entire due diligence process again. Of course, he didn't think it was a big deal because he had no idea what his team was going through, but the rest of the team did. It was awful. If you are ever selling with partners, please, don't be prideful. Don't be selfish. Don't make decisions that are just for you. People may consider you a good business manager, but truthfully, you are just being an ass. There is no amount of money out there that is big enough to screw your friends over for it. The interesting thing is that as I write this now, I think that person now knows that the advice was terrible. But at the time, it just meant a ton of stress for everyone to deal with. I love all the guys we did the deal with, but it was pushing me to my absolute limits.

In the letter of intent, a proposed or expected closing date is written down. That closing date may change throughout the diligence process. It gets pushed back for one thing or another. They may need one document that they couldn't find and now it must be pushed off a few days. Don't worry. You are hopefully just waiting on tens of millions of dollars (or even hundreds of thousands of dollars) to be deposited into your bank account. No big deal. Sure, move it a week, move it another! Yeah, no big deal. After a lot of speculation, the closing date was finally set. It was April 6th, 2023. We had to sign final documents in the days leading up to it. I was lying in bed, sick, signing the final documents via DocuSign. I remember holding up my phone so I could see the docs and signing and thinking, "Gosh, I can't believe I got sick while we are about to close." I got a call from Collin that night and he was congratulating me. I told him how frustrated I was that I was sick during this time. He told me he would get sick because of stress when he was closing deals and that it was normal. I was appreciative to have him on our side. The deal we did with Climate Control Experts not only got us a great company to work with, but it got us a terrific group of partners who had a lot of experience with deals of this size and larger. I had been a consultant on the buy side and the sell side, but doing a deal of this size for yourself is a whole different story. Collin really helped make it all happen. He was like my Sherpa or mentor, guiding me through this process.

I got up on April 6th and went to the office. Gerry, Dennis, Brent, and I were all able to cram into Dennis' small office. Gerry brought his wife and brother, and they crammed in as well. Dennis got on the Zoom call that the attorneys had set up for the closing. Everyone was on the call. Our attorneys, Service Champions Attorneys, Service Champions executives, all of us, Collin, and Dan Antonelli (who had one percent and had done all the branding for the company), and the bankers. Everyone involved was either in the small office or on the Zoom call. We all had to approve the transaction. The call was recorded, and it was surreal.

They started off with, "Dennis, are you present?"

"Yes, Dennis is present." "Dennis, are you clear to close?" "Yes, I am clear to close."

"Tom Howard, are you present...."

It went on and on, one at a time, like launching a rocket. Then, without warning, we heard the attorneys say, "This transaction is complete. The funds are authorized for transfer."

It all ended quite suddenly. The Zoom meeting ended, and we all started smiling. We looked around the room and people gave each other high fives and hugs. We had done it. We couldn't believe it.

We all left that day, and everyone was checking their phones almost every minute, refreshing every fifteen seconds, waiting to see when the funds hit the bank account. Gerry was in the parking lot of the building when his hit. He was the first one to get his funds. Mine was last. They had a hang up and mine didn't hit until four hours later. It felt like the longest four hours of my life. But it was worth the wait.

I took the rest of the day off and went out with my wife to go shopping. We were sitting in the mall. My wife was trying on shoes when the funds hit. Needless to say, the bill got a little expensive that day, but we enjoyed it before we had to take a bunch of money out for taxes, investments, and charitable giving.

Chapter Twenty-Six

THE AFTERMATH

The money was great, and we did enjoy that day and the new things we could do because of the money. But the best feeling came from the sense of accomplishment. We had gone from zero dollars ($0) to over $50 million in one year without investing a single penny. It was quite the story. As I said earlier, I cannot disclose the actual amount due to a non-disclosure agreement with the buyer but publicly published reports show roughly what the amount was around. Even without the exact sale price in mind, generating that kind of cash in that short if a time was hard for even me to believe and I lived through the whole thing.

I wrote a journal during the process and that is how this book started. I stopped halfway through while I was moving houses but I'm glad that I picked it back up to finish it. I wanted to tell other people how we did this and hopefully, my story—our story—could inspire and motivate you to do the same thing.

I am currently prepping my largest company for sale. I have a lot more equity in this one and the EBITDA is higher as well. The money will be good, but the process and doing it with your team is what builds lasting memories. I will always remember the team from Fetch.

Finally, here are the key points from this book to always remember:

- Always respect the positions of the people on your team. Never decide for them, even if you are the owner.

- Don't go cheap on software or other automations. Build for scale.

- Loose lips really do sink ships. Don't let information out about your deals before they are done.

- Your word must hold weight. If you promise someone something, even if it's not in writing, follow through with it. If you do, people will be much more willing to sell you their business or do business with you in general.

- BUILD A BUDGET. MAKE A PLAN. All the things in your company should be done in order to hit your budget. If you don't have one, then your goals are really just wishes.

- You can build something bigger and faster than you ever thought possible. Make your goals bigger and drive towards them. If you set subpar goals, you will get subpar results. I wish I had made bigger goals a lot sooner in my life.

After the sale, we each went in our own directions. Dennis and Brent continued to work at Fetch. Gerry took a role there as well but Service Champions corporate took over a lot of the marketing reducing Gerry's role. I stopped working with them as part of the agreement with the sale. I continued to work at ServiceTitan helping contractors, which is still a passion of mine to this day. I am hoping to complete my next large sale, my company Lee's Air, at the end of 2025 or early 2026. Collin and Trevor went on to sell their company, the Flint group just months after the Fetch deal was complete. They were a massive success in all their other ventures and it led to an unbelievable outcome for them as well. Finally, Dan Antonelli from Kick Charge Marketing, who had made the brand that we were all proud of, took the money from his percentage of the deal and bought a nice car and put some towards his beach house. He ended up selling part of his company to Tommy Mello from A1 garage for an undisclosed amount.

We had our trying times throughout the process, but I will always look back on that group and smile. That team pulled off something that I was delighted to be a part of.

I don't like touting what charitable things people do with their money or brag amount my own contributions there. I can tell you though that I am aware of multiple people in this group that have been very generous with their time, talents, and monetary resources to help a lot of contractors and other people by utilizing either the money or knowledge that they received from this sale. I wish you the best in whatever endeavor you are undertaking, and I sincerely hope that you will be wildly successful in it but more importantly, try to help out the next ones that want to attempt the same.

ABOUT TOM HOWARD

Tom Howard got his start in the HVAC and plumbing industry when he was fifteen years old. He was the son of a hard-working single mother, and she demanded that he get a job as soon as possible. He found one sweeping floors and cleaning trucks for a small contractor near his childhood home. His boss offered him a raise if he started taking classes in the trades and he grew from there. After high school, he served a full-time religious mission in Hungary for two years and then attended Brigham Young University and earned a degree in Finance. After college, he took a job as a general manager for an HVAC company that he would later purchase. He has bought over a dozen companies since then that are both inside and outside the trades. He still owns the first company that he purchased and, as of 2025, it completes over 100 million in revenue annually. He is a proud father of four sons and resides in Las Vegas Nevada.

www.ingramcontent.com/pod-product-compliance
Lightning Source LLC
Chambersburg PA
CBHW071551200326
41519CB00021BB/6700